Beyond the Call

Why Some of Your Team Go the Extra Mile and Others Don't Show

Marc Woods and Steve Coomber

WILEY

A John Wiley & Sons, Ltd., Publication

Cover design by Parent Design Ltd (www.parentdesign.co.uk)

Registered office
John Wiley and Sons Ltd, The Atrium, Southern Gate, Chichester, West Sussex, PO19 8SQ, United Kingdom

For details of our global editorial offices, for customer services and for information about how to apply for permission to reuse the copyright material in this book please see our website at www.wiley.com.

Wiley publishes in a variety of print and electronic formats and by print-on-demand. Some material included with standard print versions of this book may not be included in e-books or in print-on-demand. If this book refers to media such as a CD or DVD that is not included in the version you purchased, you may download this material at http://booksupport.wiley.com. For more information about Wiley products, visit www.wiley.com.

Designations used by companies to distinguish their products are often claimed as trademarks. All brand names and product names used in this book are trade names, service marks, trademarks or registered trademarks of their respective owners. The publisher is not associated with any product or vendor mentioned in this book.

Library of Congress Cataloging-in-Publication Data is available

A catalogue record for this book is available from the British Library.

ISBN 978-1-119-96258-8 (paperback) ISBN 978-1-119-96939-6 (ebk)
ISBN 978-1-119-96940-2 (ebk) ISBN 978-1-119-96941-9 (ebk)

Set in 11/14.5 pt Sabon by Toppan Best-set Premedia Limited

Printed in Great Britain by TJ International Ltd, Padstow, Cornwall

CONTENTS

FOREWORD

Why do we feel better working for some bosses, in some teams, and in some organizations, than in others? Why do we feel like giving that little bit more – going the extra mile – without counting the cost?

This great book by Marc Woods and Steve Coomber provides some powerful insights into how to create an environment that enables people to be the best they can be everyday, and go beyond the basic.

I've been privileged to work for a great company all of my career and, because I am in Human Resources, I have spent a lot of time thinking about how to create an environment and a culture that inspires people to be the best they can be . . . . every day. *Beyond the Call* captures so much of what it takes to create that environment – the importance of trust, and the role of being a leader who serves. Treating people the way they want to be treated – not just as you want to be treated – so understanding their needs and motivations. Matching the work they do to their strengths and giving meaning to why they do that work.

If people "want to", rather than "have to" or "need to" – magic happens. Giving people the freedom to make decisions, allows them to feel pride in, and ownership of, what they do – so of course they will go *beyond the call* – wouldn't you?

Jane Reay Jones
HR Manager, Procter & Gamble

Beyond the Call addresses a topic that goes to the very heart of what makes organisations successful in the 21st Century. Of course products, services, innovation, structures, operations, processes, logistics – these are all vital. But at the heart of any organisation are its people, and how much they care about the enterprise and want it to succeed really matters. That includes everyone who contributes to the network of value creation, whether they are customers, suppliers, innovation partners, employees, or shareholders.

No organisation can prescribe every action these people should take on its behalf. Yet a large part of delivering on the organisation's vision and objectives has to be down to its people. This is where discretionary effort is so important. If you have people who believe in your cause, and who will go above and beyond the call of duty, whether that it is to do with the quality of their work, the hours they do, their determination to solve problems and overcome challenges, to cope with adversity, to make customers happy, then your business is on course to exceed expectations.

This book provides a useful framework to help managers understand more about discretionary effort. It explores some of the main drivers of discretionary effort, through the eyes of practising executives, and suggests ways to create the conditions that encourage discretionary effort. And, while every organisation is different, *Beyond the Call* outlines discretionary effort principles that all managers should benefit from adopting.

Jonathan Emms
Head of Primary Care, Country Lead, Pfizer UK

1. DISCRETIONARY EFFORT AND THE CASE OF THE MYSTERIOUS MR UNDERHILL

'The difference between what we do and what we are capable of doing would suffice to solve most of the world's problem.'

Mahatma Gandhi

Like many people, I opened a bank account when I was a teenager. I still bank with the same business decades later. Relatively few people switch bank accounts. It is called customer inertia. Or status quo bias, if you are a behavioural economist. Apparently, the statistics say that divorce is more likely than changing your bank. Yet on one occasion my dealings with the bank became so difficult over such an apparently small matter, that I very nearly did this most unlikely of things.

I considered myself a good customer, and I was well served with bank accounts. I already had a current, a business and a savings account. Now, with my work regularly taking me abroad, I decided to open a foreign currency bank account as well. As a long-standing customer the initial process was straightforward and I was quickly allocated an account number. However, when my new cheque book arrived at home, I noticed one surprising feature: it had the name Mr Underhill printed on it. Not Mr Woods. I was mystified.

Never mind, I thought. This will not take long to sort out. So I called customer service:

'Yes it has the correct account number printed on it,' I responded to the bank representative.

'And you received it at your home address?'

'I did.'

'Well you must have filled in the wrong name when you originally completed the paperwork and applied for the account.'

Hmmm. Okay, I hadn't expected the operative to take personal responsibility for the mistake, but I wasn't expecting the bank to blame me either, to the point of suggesting that I had somehow forgotten my own name. And why Underhill, anyway?

Over the next few months I telephoned, emailed, faxed, telephoned, made personal appearances at my bank, and telephoned, all in an effort to fix the issue. Nothing, however, seemed to penetrate the mysterious Kafkaesque procedures of the bank. I couldn't even cancel the account. And in the meantime the letters to Mr Underhill kept arriving . . . and arriving.

So there it was. I had apparently reached an impasse. There was nothing for it. Time to bring my long-standing and, until that point, happy relationship with the bank to an end. And then, at last, an epiphany.

I was at the bank where a bank employee was processing a number of transactions for me and, as she went through the process, efficiently and politely, I commented that it was a shame that not everyone in the bank did their job as well. Showing some concern, she asked me if I'd had some issues, and so I explained the difficulties I'd had and the frustration I felt that no one seemed to want to take responsibility.

In just five minutes this helpful person ended six months of unbelievable aggravation. She wasn't sure what had caused the initial error with my new account or of the process required to fix it. She called several departments explaining that Mr Underhill really didn't exist, and she reassured colleagues that common sense should prevail, commenting to them that it was highly unlikely that it was the customer's error.

It wasn't her job, and it certainly wasn't her fault, but she fixed the problem anyway and retained a customer. She went beyond the call of duty. She went the extra mile.

Some months later I was doing some work for the same bank and shared the story with a senior director. He was mortified that their processes had failed and that their staff had let both the business and me down. I told him that he had at least one employee he could be proud of. And I told him her name and where she worked.

This person wasn't expecting any reward when she helped me, and I'm sure this level of customer service wasn't an isolated incident, but six months later I was delighted to hear that she had been promoted.

Roman taxis

Many people will recognize the phrase, 'to go the extra mile'. A few will know that the phrase has its origins in the Bible, and in particular the Sermon on the Mount. At the time, around 28BC, your average, feeling slightly puffed out Roman centurion, could compel a random passer-by to carry the centurion's belongings for a *mille passuum* – 1000 paces – also known as a Roman mile. Understandably, people were not that happy at having to take an unplanned detour as a human taxi, carrying someone else's belongings. Hence the resonance of the part of the sermon where Jesus, according to Matthew 5:41, advises onlookers: 'If anyone forces you to go one mile, go with them two miles.'

Over the centuries the phrase 'going the extra mile' has become common parlance for doing that little bit (or a lot) extra, going out of your way to be helpful. Just as the employee at the bank had, thankfully, in the case of the mysterious Mr Underhill.

Until my unfortunate experience with the bank, I had given little thought to the notion of going the extra mile. But, having suffered the frustrations of organizational bureaucracy, at first hand, as well as the redeeming power of employee intervention, I began to give the idea more consideration. I paid much more attention to interactions with shop staff. I listened to the way call centre staff dealt with my queries when I needed to speak to them. I observed the way that airline, hotel, restaurant and other service centred employees treated me when I was travelling. And, in particular, I asked other people that I met in the course of my work to tell me about any relevant or related experiences in business.

So, for example, I learnt about the document delivery company where the manager of the local branch has a customer living some distance from the nearest mail collection point, but in the same village as the manager. And every evening the manager drops the customer's post off for them. The manager doesn't have to. They just do.

In that same company, people often go out of their way to stop by a person's house to pick up an item if that customer has missed a collection. And, in extreme winter weather conditions one year, with numerous communities snowed in across the UK, the business managed to keep its operations running; partly because people made the effort, often to their detriment, to get to the company's premises to pick up the mail. In fact, in some instances, it was more of a challenge to stop employees coming in to work, as the weather was so desperate that the firm wasn't sure it would be able to get its lorries back out of the depot.

As one company member described it: 'If something is happening, they will pick up the situation, they will own it. It doesn't even matter if it is on a weekend, in the middle of the night, whatever it is, this really isn't a company where you just put your shoes on, turn up at nine o'clock and go home at five.'

Leveraging your human capital

It is easy to see why the idea of employees going the extra mile might interest senior executives, and other managers in organizations. Over the last few years, businesses have battled through some of the toughest trading conditions since World War II. Possibly the most difficult. Many of the developed western economies are overburdened with debt. Attempts to deleverage have weighed heavily on economic and corporate growth. The debt crisis in Greece and fears over the indebtedness of other European countries, for example, has had a negative impact on sentiment both in the Eurozone and further afield.

Over the decades business has been through distinct stages of competition. Back in the early 20th century, companies competed using mass production techniques – interchangeable parts, continuous assembly lines, and division of labour – to produce high volumes of standardized products. Millions of identical Ford Model-T automobiles rolled out of the Highland Park plant in Michigan, for example. And, from 1914 onwards, they were available in any colour you wanted, so long as it was black. Later on, product variation, marketing and branding became more important factors in obtaining competitive advantage. More recently companies have sought to beat their rivals on price, outsourcing elements of the value chain, and through knowledge and innovation – in the so-called knowledge economy.

Today, it is widely accepted that human capital is one of the most valuable assets an organization possesses. Increasingly it is the quality of the people working in the organization that determines whether it outperforms its competitors and succeeds or fails. Not the price of its products, its manufacturing techniques, or its distribution network – although these are all an important part of the competitive mix.

Organizations are doing business in highly competitive global markets. They rely on the efforts of their staff to build and maintain relationships with their stakeholders, including their customers. Employees have a significant role to play in creating customer loyalty. Talented staff are the catalyst for change in organizations, they help detect threatening market signals, and reshape business models through innovation. An organization's people are the key to competitive survival and its ability to evolve and create sustainable success.

Capitalizing on human capital is not easy, though. For a start there is the challenge of attracting talented people. It is over a decade since global management consultants McKinsey, predicted a war for talent in business. That prediction has come true, and on a huge scale. Today, the talent wars are waged globally. Even at times of high unemployment, many firms still say that they cannot get the right mix of talented people that they need. Most organizations have acknowledged the importance of human capital, in driving innovation, organizational effectiveness and competitiveness. Many have developed a strong focus on recruiting, nurturing, developing and retaining talent. Some have appointed specialist officers – chief talent managers.

The idea that organizations could unlock additional effort from their people, can play an important role in leveraging an organization's human capital. For example, when people want to do that little bit extra it sends the right signal to potential recruits. If people are willing to go the extra mile in an organization it suggests that they are happy with their work. Personal fulfilment through work seems particularly important for the most recent generations to enter the workplace.

This was brought home to me during one particular dinner in 2010 that I had with a senior partner from a large financial services firm. My dining companion explained to me how their firm had missed its target of graduate intake numbers. For this firm it was an extremely unusual event. Given the depressed jobs market I assumed that this must have been because the company were unable to find enough graduates of the quality that they were looking for. But apparently not. Instead, the hiring dynamic had changed. The graduates were, in effect, interviewing the financial services firm, and many graduates decided that what this firm had to offer did not match their expectations.

These young people were prepared and expecting to work hard for their eventual employer. But not unconditionally. They wanted the business to explain to them why they should give their precious time to this company, and not to another organization. It seemed to me then – and still does – that if an organization could show that the people in the organization were fulfilled enough in their work to want to go the extra mile, it would persuade more graduates to sign up. (In conjunction with a clearly thought out CSR programme and a well signposted career pathway, that is.)

Not forgetting the need to get the most out of the existing workforce. Against a backdrop of stalling economic growth at best, and stagnation recession at worst, organizations are reducing headcounts, cutting overtime, and limiting worked hours, as they pare back costs. Few organizations are hiring in any number. At these times, more than any perhaps, organizations need every talented person they employ contributing at their maximum.

And there are many other benefits. A good example is the innovation impact. Innovation is another route to competitive advantage. Traditional in-house research and development is no longer enough to confer competitive advantage on firms. The pace of change is too quick, the resources required to make significant breakthroughs often too great for individual organizations to bear. Instead, companies are embracing cross-boundary networked innovation with a range of innovation partners. Here again, individuals who are willing to go beyond the compass of their normal activities – in order to search out novel value propositions, and build innovation relationships – are highly sought after and valuable to the firm.

Action beyond engagement

There is a specific term to describe the idea of additional employee input – Discretionary Effort – although it is a relatively unexplored concept in academic research literature. Of course discretionary effort has always existed. When the master craftsman employed by Egyptian Pharaoh Khufu was giving the marble casing stones covering the Great Pyramid of Giza a little extra shine in 2560BC, he didn't realize he was dispensing 'discretionary effort' as such.

And so it has been ever since. In the meantime the management literature has picked up on associated ideas like employee engagement – very popular with HR directors more recently – while discretionary effort, a key employee behaviour, remains comparatively unchartered territory.

For a sense check, I canvassed the opinions of numerous senior executives, many in very well-known organizations. Was discretionary effort a concept they recognized? How important was it? The majority of responses backed up my hunch that this was an area well worth further investigation.

'Do I think it's important?' said one executive I spoke to, in a huge global organization. 'I think it's very important, and I would say, in our organization, we almost assume it. The organization relies on it and counts on it, and it's a source of competitive advantage. If you've got people who believe in a cause and will go above and beyond, whether it is hours worked, quality, determination when things go wrong, what-ever form it takes, it's crucial. When I recruit people, that's what I'm looking for. It's as important as IQ, EQ, skills and competencies. So you look for it. When it's missing, it really shows.'

Or, as a senior manager in a large global business service organization explained: 'I think it's absolutely essential. Without discretionary effort, I think most organizations would have major problems, and I think it's both a differentiator and it's increasingly an essential. Thinking of our own organization, the number of potentially tricky situations that we get into, that we then get out of, consistently, because either people or teams go the extra mile, it's phenomenal. If we didn't have people that were prepared to give discretionary effort, then we'd be failing as an organization. The number of times that it's a special effort, an extra effort, that makes a difference for our customer, and either remedies the situation, or wins a piece of revenue. It happens every day. So you can't do without it.'

A small number of organizations both recognized the importance of the concept and were taking steps to see if they could find ways of encouraging employees to give discretionary effort, or at least make it easier for them to do so. This might, for example, be tied to their existing employee engagement policies in some way. Or it may be connected to the company's values and vision, or other of its HR practices.

Some organizations linked the concept to their Corporate Social Responsibility agenda. Others were unfamiliar with the term, but thought the idea was a valuable one. As one person said: 'As a leader or manager of people, I've always tried to make sure that those people are working to their maximum potential, and then some. But I guess I've never really thought about it as discretionary effort.'

People power

Clearly, discretionary effort is a topic that deserves greater attention. After all, imagine if all employees behaved like the woman in the bank who finally fixed my problem, or the company employees who battled through the snow and ice to make their deliveries. How powerful would that be? How much would that boost the reputation of a company? Think how it would raise performance across an organization.

Unfortunately, in most organizations, not everyone behaves this way. As many managers will recognize, getting some people to do even the simplest tasks is like pulling teeth, whilst other individuals surprise you with their passion and desire to deliver more than expected. One bunch of employees will go the extra mile for the business, are a pleasure to work with, and provide an extraordinary customer experience, yet others do just as much as is expected of them and not a bit more, or even less if they can get away with it.

These were the kinds of comments I heard repeatedly on my business travels supporting organizations at their leadership, sales and training events. The stories were in many different forms. They were told by people working in different sized companies, in dissimilar industries, across continents, in all kinds of functions and roles. Yet, despite their differences, the tale that they told was a broadly similar one.

Yes – there were people in their organization that frequently went the extra mile at work, while others didn't. Why was that? What makes the difference between semi-reluctant compliance and willing extra effort?

Engagement, discretionary effort and coercion

It is important at this point to distinguish discretionary effort from employee engagement, a concept many companies have begun to take more seriously over the last decade. Commissioning an employee engagement survey to determine how engaged your workforce is, is a fairly common practice in organizations these days. Many of the companies I spoke to do a lot of work around employee engagement.

Invariably, employee engagement survey findings confirm that the majority of employees are fairly engaged in the business. Great news for the organization in question. And usually the survey results also reveal that there are some areas that could be improved on, which in turn would increase employee engagement. Yet often there remains a sense that employees could contribute a lot more. That they want to contribute more, but maybe there is something holding them back.

It makes sense that organizations take measures to improve employee engagement. But maybe engagement is not the complete picture. What if employee engagement doesn't necessarily translate into productive useful action and behaviour? It seems perfectly possible to have an individual who is highly engaged in an organization, and yet does nothing more than what's already asked of them. The components which drive engagement do not necessarily encourage or lead to additional effort.

Discretionary effort is different. What if we could identify specific drivers that feed into discretionary effort; the factors that encourage people to go the extra mile? Then organizations could act on those drivers. For a start, they could measure their performance with respect to the different drivers of discretionary effort. They could identify those drivers where their scores were below par, and that would allow them to focus on improving those particular drivers. Equally, they would be able to identify areas where their performance was already strong and required less attention.

As well as identifying the drivers of discretionary effort it should be possible to construct a way of assessing an organization's overall discretionary performance. Then that organization could be benchmarked itself against other organizations, both in the same sector and outside.

I should emphasise at this point that I'm not interested in coercing people to do more. Of course it is often possible to squeeze a little bit extra from people under duress. But while the threat of the stick – whether it relates to job security or reward or remuneration – may work for a while, it is no recipe for creating a high performing organization. For most managers, it's neither desirable, nor sustainable. So it is not a question of *forcing* more from your people, and in the current difficult economic climate, organizations probably could not force much more from their staff anyway, even if they tried.

I'm also less interested in the direct encouragement of people to do more than usual through overt rewards, such as bonuses, prizes, rewards for targets and so on; although these definitely have their place in maximizing an organization's performance.

What I am interested in is whether it is possible to create the conditions within an organization that mean that people will do more than they are asked to, of their own volition. They behave in ways that go over and above the behaviour they are mandated to display. They do that little bit (or a lot) extra, without the overt promise of some organizational reward. In short, they give discretionary effort because they want to.

A different perspective on performance

I'm not alone in thinking that by improving the environments in which people work, we can improve performance – both for the individual and organization – over a range of measures. Or that some of the metrics we use to determine an organization's performance, particularly some of the hard financial data, are not necessarily the most suitable for this purpose. In fact, when it comes to thinking about the well-being of a workforce, or a nation even, I'm in good company. Increasingly, policymakers and practitioners are engaging in a new debate, looking beyond the numbers when considering what constitutes success, whether that is at the level of the organization or national economy.

In France, for example, the government has been investigating ways to shift from measuring economic production to measuring well-being as a determinant of the prosperity of a nation. The government in the United Kingdom has also moved to include questions about happiness and well-being in the national household survey conducted by the UK's Office of National Statistics. And then there is the kingdom of Bhutan in the Himalayas, which has been measuring its nation's Gross National Happiness since the 1970s.

The recognition of academic excellence also reflects this change in thinking and attitudes. For example, Daniel Kahneman, a psychologist at Princeton University in the US, was awarded the Nobel Prize, partly for his expertise in hedonic psychology – studying what makes us happy or sad.

With this book I hope to add to the debate about how best to improve performance in organizations, and the wider economy. By focusing on discretionary effort and the factors that make discretionary effort more likely, *Beyond the Call* will enable organizations to create the conditions where people want to give their best at work, rather than just turning up because they have to. It provides organizations with the tools to achieve greater success, and with new ways of thinking about and measuring performance.

2. A MANIFESTO FOR DISCRETIONARY EFFORT

'The only thing of real importance that leaders do is to create and manage culture'

Edgar Schein, professor emeritus MIT Sloan School of Management

In today's organizations, perhaps more than ever before, people matter. Call it human capital if you like. But what we are really talking about are the employees that make up an organization, and all the other people whose actions contribute to that organization's success. The evidence suggests that employees are currently able to do a lot more than they are doing at work. What stops them from doing that little bit extra? Often it is the environment that they are working in, the culture of the organization that they work for, and the nature of their relationship with their manager, organization, and the other people they work with.

Our research and this book aim to go some way to closing the discretionary effort gap – between what people are potentially prepared to do and what they actually do. I want this book to be of practical use to organizations. Much of the book is focused on the key drivers of discretionary effort, where organizations can really make a difference. And while you will find some theory in the following pages, I have focused on drawing out some of the most important practical aspects related to each driver.

In doing so, I have tapped into the knowledge, expertise and opinions of the people actually coping with the realities of doing business in the current business environment – whether providing services or products, delivering budgets, increasing revenues, cutting costs or making a profit. What better way to explore the issues associated with discretionary effort than through the ideas, actions and experiences of these individuals?

The leaders I spoke to about discretionary effort are convinced that it is an important management topic. In particular, the concept appeared to offer a route to improved performance for organizations.

But while anecdotal evidence about the importance of discretionary effort can be persuasive, it needs to be placed on sounder footings. How do you define discretionary effort, for example? What other concepts are similar? What are the constituent elements of discretionary effort? Does an individual's motivation for going the extra mile matter?

If organizations could put themselves in a position to assess easily their discretionary effort performance, by identifying areas where performance was outstanding, adequate, or poor, then it would be possible to suggest ways to create an environment where discretionary effort was likely to flourish. In other words, an environment where people wanted to work, were more productive in doing so, and more inclined to give their best.

Not that it is easy. Much of this is about cultural change and that takes time, and is often met with resistance. So, for example, you need the right people to see it through, discretionary effort champions, and the right incentives for it to happen.

As one person said to me: 'Everything in my experience that creates discretionary effort is about a company's culture, and that can be set, it can be adjusted, it can be modified, but it can also be ignored if you have the wrong sorts of managers in place. And you have to set a tone that encourages people to enjoy and get some sort of personal satisfaction from discretionary effort.'

Remember, too, that this is not a cynical exercise in manipulating people to do more for less. Primarily, I want to give people what they want from a working environment. Whether or not they then do more than they are asked to, is incidental. However, there is every chance that given the 'right' working environment that supports discretionary effort, people will go the extra mile.

A solid foundation

At this point I could have set out on my own to find out more about discretionary effort. But I decided that it was a topic that deserved more thorough investigation. And so I decided to commission some professional academic research to provide a solid foundation for discussing the subject.

To help with the research I turned to Dr Christopher Rotolo. Christopher – in his own words – is an industrial-organizational psychologist with over 20 years of experience 'assisting organizations in aligning their human assets with their business strategies and processes.' He is an adjunct associate professor in New York University's psychology department where he teaches organizational climate and culture, and human resources selection.

He has worked extensively with Fortune 50 companies, as well as local and Federal governments in the US in the areas of organizational diagnosis and development, cultural due diligence, turnover analysis, social network analysis, employee satisfaction surveys, assessment centres, multi-source assessment and feedback, and executive development.

After some discussion Chris assembled a team of master's students from NYU's organizational psychology department to help with the research. The NYU industrial and organizational psychology faculty is very well-regarded, ranking in the top five US psychology PhD programmes according to the *Princeton Review's* Gourman Report of Graduate Programmes (8th ed.).

The initial plan was: to research the concept of discretionary effort, examine the previous research on this and associated concepts; construct a model of discretionary effort; create a survey that would determine a company's score across a number of drivers of discretionary effort; and then have a number of organizations from a variety of sectors and geographies complete the survey.

The team began by postulating a definition for discretionary effort as: 'the effort that employees choose to exert in service to themselves, their co-workers, or their companies'. The willingness of the employees to perform above and beyond their job description – the call of duty – is a reflection of committing their discretionary effort. It remains the definition I use today.

Preliminary literature research revealed that the academic origin of the concept of discretionary effort (DE) stems from work by social scientist Daniel Yankelovich, a celebrated market and public policy researcher, and president and cofounder of Public Agenda, a US based non-profit research organization, and his colleague John Immerwahr, professor of philosophy at Villanova University, and also a senior research fellow at Public Agenda. In their 1983 publication, *Putting the Work Ethic to Work* (Public Agenda Foundation) Yankelovich and Immerwahr conducted an investigation into the American work ethic and its links to America's economic vitality, using interviews with 845 working Americans, as well as looking at comparative studies conducted elsewhere in the world, including the UK and Japan.

In their report, Yankelovich and Immerwahr suggest that employees were applying as little as 30 per cent of the total effort that they are able to, towards doing their job. In other words, 70 per cent of employee effort remained untapped. A later survey in 1996, *A Study of Voluntary Effort in the Workplace*, by Response Analysis in Princeton New Jersey, for consultants Blessing White, revealed that only 39% of respondents said that their organizations did a good job (29%), or a very good job (10%) of encouraging voluntary effort.

Consequently, the research team then looked at a bunch of concepts that appeared to be of some use in helping to understand and work towards a model of discretionary effort. So, for example, the team looked at organizational citizenship behaviour (OCB), a concept attributed to Dennis Organ, professor of management at the Kelley School of Business, Indiana University. Organ described OCB in *Organizational Citizenship Behaviour: The good soldier syndrome* (1988) as, 'individual behaviour that is discretionary, not directly or explicitly recognized by the formal reward system, and that in the aggregate promotes the effective functioning of the organization.'

The researchers also unearthed other ideas that appeared related to discretionary effort. These included extra-role behaviour – behaviour by an employee that both attempts to benefit the organization, as well as going further than expected of them in their the role. This is not behaviour that is prescribed by the role, recognized by formal reward systems, or punished if is not performed. Or prosocial behaviour – where a person voluntarily exhibits behaviour that they expect to benefit someone else, without expecting anything in return. These are positive social acts intended to create and maintain the well-being and integrity of others. Cooperating, donating, helping, sharing, and volunteering are all forms of prosocial behaviour.

And, finally, another area that seemed useful was work engagement (this is different from employee engagement). The concept includes a behavioural component made up of behaviours such as demonstrating initiative, proactively seeking opportunities to contribute, and going beyond what is typically expected or required. These obviously chime with our idea of discretionary effort. Factors feeding into work engagement include: personality characteristics; conscientiousness as a trait; job tasks; autonomy; the variety and challenge of work; the conditions surrounding working, including the attributes of the work – the boss, the availability of resources, co-workers, and career progress issues; and trust.

Having trawled through what little existing literature there was on the subject, and identifying these associated ideas, it was soon clear that there was very little research on discretionary effort as such, and certainly not on the components of discretionary effort as a behaviour or phenomenon.

Towards a model of discretionary effort

The research team's next steps were to take the different concepts the literature review unearthed and, after much discussion, hypothesize some possible models of discretionary effort. In arriving at these suggested models the team explored and debated a number of different elements that seemed to be important dimensions of discretionary effort.

So, for example, while organizational citizenship behaviour was clearly similar to the suggested definition of discretionary effort in some respects, there seemed to be important differences. While organizational citizenship behaviours are made without self-interest or self-purpose it was entirely feasible that discretionary effort could be motivated by selfish reasons.

It also seemed plausible that it might be possible to distinguish between different types of discretionary effort. So, for example, maybe discretionary effort could be divided up into that extra effort given within the employee's existing role (in-role discretionary effort) or outside the employee's role (extra-role discretionary effort).

Here, in-role discretionary effort is defined as 'putting effort in beyond the expected level within one's job description, while neither punished for its absence nor directly rewarded, and with or without a personal purpose'. So some examples of this include: voluntarily putting in extra hours to achieve a result faster; working after hours to get tasks done; coming up with original ideas for handling work; and having a work attendance record considerably above the average.

Then, for extra-role Discretionary Effort, the team used the definition of: 'putting effort in beyond one's job description while neither punished for its absence nor directly rewarded, and with or without a personal purpose. Examples of this include: training people to perform their job better; volunteering to things that are not formally required by the job; helping out others when they have heavy workloads or work related problems; and making suggestions to improve the organization.

This might be important, for example, if an organization wanted to create the conditions where employers would do more of what they were meant to be doing already. Or, alternatively, an organization wanted to prompt discretionary effort from employees to be directed outside of their existing role.

Another possible dimension of distinction the team looked at was who or what discretionary effort was directed towards. The team identified three possibilities:

1. Towards the individual themselves (DE-self – DE-S). So, for example, this might include actions intended to gain recognition, or make the individual feel good about themselves when helping others.
2. Towards other people (DE-others, DE-O), when behaviour is altruistic, for example.
3. Towards the company (DE-company, DE-C).

As we began to construct a more concrete model, in addition to looking at the broader context and scope of discretionary effort and its possible dimensions, the team also discussed the possible drivers of discretionary effort in more detail. In doing this they continued to draw on both the ideas thrown up by the literature review, as well as the team's own thoughts and ideas on the topic.

The drivers were divided into four distinct groups depending on their connection with one of the areas of behaviour or activity: leadership, organizational environment, work engagement and personality.

Internal

Drivers ↕ ⟶ Discretionary ⟶ Outcomes
Effort

External

Internal Drivers	External Drivers	Outcomes
Personality	**Organizational Environment**	- Group Cohesiveness
- Agreeableness	- Structure & Procedure	- Net Promoter
- Conscientiousness	- Team Identification	- Sick Days/Paid Vacation
	- Company Trustworthiness	- Quality of Performance
Work Engagement		- Performance Management
- Vigour	**Leadership**	- Recent Bonus/Merits/Recognition
- Dedication	- Trustworthiness	- Commitment
- Absorption	- Individualized Consideration	- Job Satisfaction
	- Empowerment	
	- Autonomy	
	- Self-Sacrificing	
	- Clarity	
	- Charismatic Leadership	

Figure 2.1

(The complete set of drivers: Agreeableness, Conscientiousness, Vigour, Dedication, Absorption, Structure & Procedure,
Team Identification, Company Trustworthiness, Trustworthiness, Individualized Consideration, Empowerment, Autonomy, Self-Sacrificing, Clarity, Charismatic Leadership. Not all
of these were used in the final model, however. See the section
on drivers later in this chapter.)

Testing the model

The research team then conducted a multi-company study
with companies from a variety of industries and from public,
private and non-government sectors. These included a number
of companies with a market capitalization of over $100
billion, including a number of Fortune 500 and FTSE 100
companies. Data was collected through a web-based questionnaire given to employees. A series of closed and open-
ended questions were answered, by over 900 respondents, as

well as several scales that assessed the attitudes, behaviours and certain predispositions of the respondents.

In addition, my writing partner and I spoke to a number of people across different organizations, both non-profit and for-profit, to explore issues around establishing the drivers of discretionary effort. Many of these were senior executives in large, often well-known, organizations. The majority of executives interviewed held positions of vice president or higher within companies with a combined market capital of over $675 billion. These included chairmen, CEOs and presidents with responsibilities for organizations with a combined market capital of $12 billion. In addition there were senior HR directors with total responsibilities for over 130,000 employees, and heads of engagement with responsibilities for 168,000 employees. Some of these conversations were in the form of extensive in-depth interviews, while others were briefer exchanges.

The people we spoke to deal with the challenges associated with leading and managing people in organizations on a daily basis. With these executives I discussed the practical day-to-day challenges and solutions that were encountered in their work, as well as their experiences and thoughts about the drivers that the research identified. While some of these people worked for organizations that participated in the quantitative research, others did not. All worked for organizations that were performing relatively well in difficult circumstances. I attach considerable value to their opinions, as in most instances they have considerable experience of succeeding in organizations, regardless of sector.

The drivers

The research revealed that most of the drivers in our suggested model correlated with discretionary effort. At the same time, the combined scores from the questionnaire suggest that organizations have plenty of room for improvement. The average percentage of the workforce giving discretionary effort was 61%. When employees do go the extra mile it is most often to help their colleagues (83%) or to further the interests of the company (70%). Interestingly, going the extra mile for selfish interests – in anticipation of some kind of reward, for example, is far less common (37%).

Organizations as a whole scored below 70% for a number of drivers including empowerment, individualized consideration and sacrificial leadership, for example. But it was on procedural justice (44%) and company trustworthiness (58%) where organizations performed particularly poorly.

Besides considering the drivers in the context of the four distinct groups – leadership, organizational environment, work engagement and personality – the drivers can be divided into two categories overall – internal and external drivers – and within these, into a number of sub-groups.

Internal drivers

Internal drivers stem from a person's individual characteristics. They may, for example, be partly determined genetically. It is also likely that, while not completely impossible, organizations have limited ability to influence these drivers.

One group of internal drivers relates to personality; in particular, agreeableness and conscientiousness. These are two of the so-called 'Big Five' factors of personality, a concept dating back to the 1960s and subsequently developed further by various academics. People who are agreeable tend to be considerate, empathetic, friendly and helpful. Altruism is associated with agreeableness, for example. While conscientious people are painstaking and careful, hard-working and reliable.

Another group of internal drivers comes under the overall heading of work engagement. This is a positive, fulfilling, work-related state of mind characterized by an individual's vigour, dedication and absorption. Here, vigour relates to high levels of energy and mental resilience while working, as well as a willingness to invest effort in work, and to persist in the face of difficulty. Dedication is a sense of significance, enthusiasm, inspiration, pride and challenge. While absorption is the state of mind where in individual concentrates on and is absorbed in their work, so time flies by.

In this book I have chosen not to focus on those drivers where there is more limited ability for organizations to be able to influence the drivers, and thereby influence the discretionary effort in the organization. This includes the internal drivers. Instead, I concentrate on the drivers where organizations are easily (and less easily) able to take action that leads to substantial improvements.

Understandably, it is more difficult to affect internal drivers within an organization, particularly as they are bound up with personality characteristics. And so they are not covered in any detail in the following chapters.

This is not, however, to underestimate the importance of these drivers. Indeed, the internal drivers play a significant part in bringing about discretionary effort. The good news for organizations is that they can and should focus on maximizing the presence of these drivers during the recruitment process. There are several tests, for both the personality and work engagement drivers, which can be used to assess potential hires. Organizations can also make some impact on the work engagement drivers by focusing on job resources such as performance feedback, task variety, job design and opportunities for learning and development.

Equally, when it comes to aspects of work engagement there are other measures that may influence levels of work engagement. For example, there are likely to be links between stress in individuals and energy levels. Thus minimizing stress, through well-being programmes, working patterns – such as the availability of flexible working, and workload management, such as improving delegation skills, may improve energy levels. Or fostering a sense of pride, through employer branding, for example, may increase dedication.

However, it is with the external drivers in the next section that the organization's main opportunities lie, to create a culture and environment that supports discretionary effort.

External drivers

The second type of driver of discretionary effort is the external driver. External drivers are those which the organization is more capable of influencing, whether that is through training and development, cultural change, or rethinking operational processes and practices. As with the internal drivers, some of the external drivers identified by the team, are not easily affected by organizations. This is true of charisma, for example, which I believe most people would say is not something easily acquired through training, instruction, or other interventions. Some people are just charismatic.

This book focuses on six drivers within this category, with each explored in far more detail in its own chapter in the middle section of this book.

1. Autonomy
2. Individualized consideration
3. Self-sacrificial leadership
4. Procedural justice

5. Team identification
6. Trustworthiness

Following the conversations with practitioners, it was also apparent that a seventh external driver – clarity – appeared to be important across the majority of the other external drivers, and so rather than discuss it as a separate driver, it is considered throughout the chapters.

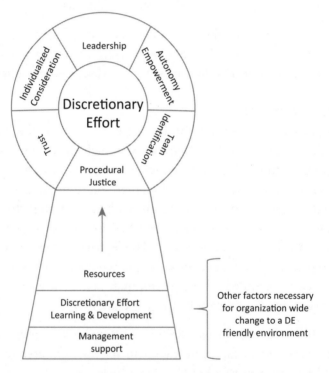

Figure 2.2 DE Driver Keyhole Model

While terms like 'procedural justice' may seem a little inaccessible, the concepts behind these drivers are comparatively simple and relate to issues that every manager and leader will recognize and have encountered at some point. These are the areas where organizations can most easily take action and that have a direct impact on enabling and encouraging people to go beyond the call of duty.

Autonomy/empowerment: The word 'autonomy' derives from the Greek 'auto' – or self – and 'nomos' – law. In other words, to self-govern. Employees who have more autonomy are more likely to act freely to benefit others, perform a greater breadth of tasks than others, and are also more likely to expand their role. There are, however, challenges for organizations that want to provide employees with more autonomy. These relate to issues such as guidance and boundary setting, striking the right balance between freedom and control, and providing the appropriate support for empowered employees.

Self-sacrificial leadership: Self-sacrificial leadership is where a leader gives up personal interest and gain for the benefit of the collective good. Acting as role models, whether intentionally or not, these leaders inspire and motivate followers to behave in a similar manner, and to provide discretionary effort. Promoting self-sacrificial leadership, however, may require changes in the way organizations, approach the performance measurement and management of individuals, and reward systems.

Individualized consideration: This is a major part of transformational leadership theory. Individualized consideration is about understanding and fulfilling the needs of followers, and treating them as individuals when doing so. This might seem relatively easy if dealing with a small team, but how do you even begin to make thousands of individuals in a multinational company, spread over several continents, feel that they are cared about as individuals?

*Procedural justice (**structure & procedure**):* How employees perceive the fairness of decision making and the way that they are treated in an organization has a strong influence on their behaviour. In particular, it affects their willingness or otherwise to give discretionary effort. Procedural justice is also an important factor in group engagement and determining whether an individual socially identifies with a particular group. Creating a fair organization, however, may involve tough decisions about openness and transparency, and difficult shifts in organizational culture.

Team identification: This driver concerns an individual's sense of belonging to a group. The more that individuals identify with the group and share its goals and values the more likely they are to go beyond the call of duty. Yet the reality of modern working life, with globalization and remote and culturally diverse teams, present real challenges in creating team identity.

Trustworthiness: Trust is a social construct which, in this case, can be defined as a willingness to have confidence in the words and actions of others, and ascribe good intentions to others. High levels of trust are associated with helping and extra-role behaviours. How do you get people to trust each other though, or the wider world to trust the organization?

Discretionary effort drives improved performance

The research shows that there is a clear business case for focusing on discretionary effort. Based on the professional analysis of the data collected from employees in the research and a review of relevant scientific facts from empirical studies, it is clear that organizations can: reduce inefficiencies; achieve better performance in certain areas; and differentiate their performance from competitors by encouraging employees' discretionary effort.

Discretionary effort correlated significantly with important company outcomes, such as group cohesiveness and quality of performance. By digging into the dimensions of discretionary effort, it's also clear that discretionary effort directed towards the company contributes the most to the company outcomes. Yet this is an area where there is considerable scope for improvement, as only 63% of respondents provide effort beyond what is required aimed at benefitting the concerns of the company, whereas 83% say that they do so to benefit their co-workers.

The team tested discretionary effort against a number of important performance metrics. In particular we looked for the impact of discretionary effort on: group cohesiveness; net promoter score; sick days and paid vacation; the quality of performance; performance management; recent bonuses, merits, and recognition; commitment; and job satisfaction.

The results were very exciting. An increase in discretionary effort positively correlates with an increase in the basket of important metrics that we looked at, many relating to performance. When you compare those organizations that had high discretionary effort scores against those with low discretionary effort scores, the high discretionary effort organizations score significantly higher on commitment, satisfaction, net promoter, performance management, and number of merits/recognition.

Also, the higher the discretionary effort score, the less likely employees are to take fake sick days, the higher their self-reported performance scores, and the greater their formal recognition in the workplace.

Closing the gap – a manifesto for discretionary effort

People spend a significant proportion of their life at work. The American Bureau of Labor Statistics found that people between the ages of 25 and 54 work 8.6 hours per day on average, for example. And sometimes it feels like a whole lot more. I believe that we have a responsibility to make sure that the experience of work is as pleasant and as fun as possible, so long as it does not have a negative impact on performance. And, if anything, research suggests that the more we enjoy our work, the better we will do it.

It may not be easy to make all work enjoyable; it seems much of it is inescapably mundane. However, in attending to the drivers of discretionary effort, organizations should also be improving their employees' appreciation and enjoyment of work. Contributing to their fulfillment as individuals. After all, those employees who have low job satisfaction are less likely to exhibit discretionary effort.

This book can be seen as a manifesto for discretionary effort, founded on the model of discretionary effort we have developed and the principles embodied in the drivers. It is not a guaranteed blueprint for organizational success – if only life were that easy. Nor is it, I suspect, a logically faultless exposition of how to improve the drivers of discretionary effort. This topic is still an emerging area, and there will be many interesting discussions along the way. However, I am passionate about creating great working environments and cultures, principled and effective leaders, great teams, and fulfilled employees. And I am sure that, if people engage with these ideas, this book will go some way towards helping that happen.

3. FREE TO DECIDE

'We figured that people will accomplish more,' he said,
'if they [the employees] are given an opportunity to use
their talents and abilities in the way they work best.'

Dave Packard

Choosing your boss

During the 1980s, as business was getting to grips with a personal computing revolution, one company in Brazil was fomenting a revolution of a different kind. Ricardo Semler took over the family business Semler & Co. in 1980. Semler was on the verge of leaving at the time, frustrated at his father's unwillingness to give up his authority. But, at the last minute, Semler's father decided to hand over control of the business to his son. He then set off for a break with the words: 'whatever changes you want to make in the organization, do them now.'

Semler noted his father's words, fired 60 per cent of the management team in the first week, and set about engineering a radical implementation of industrial democracy. Determined to remove any hint of autocratic control under his leadership, the measures carried out over the next few years went far beyond any usual steps to empower the workforce. To start with, Semler restructured the organization basing it on small teams, where each team was responsible for its own budgets and its own targets.

But this was just the beginning. Faced with a recession in the 1990s, Semco embarked on a round of cost cutting, but in agreement with the employees. Management took a substantial pay cut. And while other wages were also cut, productivity bonuses were increased, and the employees were given the power to approve, or reject, all company expenditure.

Emboldened by the responsible attitude of the employees during this period Semler restructured the company once more. The small teams remained, but this time based along product lines, and with even more autonomy. Now the employees were able to take decisions on hiring and firing. They chose their boss, and managers were rated and the results posted up for everyone to see. The employees even set their own salaries.

Pushing the concept of empowerment and autonomy even further, when it appeared as if valued employees were going to leave the company, Semler encouraged them to set up satellite businesses. A deal was structured that allowed the employee to use Semco's resources to set up their own business, and in turn Semco would receive a small payment. At one point, the satellites were contributing more than 60 per cent of the firm's business.

The revolution in industrial democracy seemed to pay off. During the 1990s Semco had managed a sevenfold increase in productivity and fivefold increase in profits. Perhaps what is most encouraging, however, is the fact that Semler's industrial experiments proved sustainable.

Freedom from the micro managers

Semco is one of the most extreme cases of empowerment and autonomy in the workplace. For most organizations such measures would be impractical or difficult to implement. But it shows what is possible when people are given greater authority and responsibility to make decisions, when they have permission to act freely to benefit and help others, and act in ways that improve the lives of others.

The evidence of countless employee engagement surveys and other research suggests that people perform better when they are not micro managed, preferring not to have someone constantly watching over their shoulder.

Things didn't start out so well at the beginning of the 20th century when Frederick Taylor's scientific management methods were all the rage. Taylorism was highly prescriptive. Taylor began his career as an engineer, and over the years developed his theory of how work could be made more productive and efficient. His ideas, captured in his 1911 book, *The Principles of Scientific Management*, centred on command and control management. The recipe for improved performance was simple: find some people who are good at a particular task; analyze the way they perform that task, breaking it down into discrete operations and actions; use a stop watch to find out the quickest way of doing these actions, and get rid of unnecessary actions; make sure everyone adopts this way of working.

It's safe to presume that Taylor was no fan of employee autonomy or empowerment. 'Hardly a competent workman can be found who does not devote a considerable amount of time to studying just how slowly he can work and still convince his employer that he is going at a good pace,' is one of his more famous sayings. Or: 'Brutally speaking, our scheme does not ask any initiative in a man. We do not care for his initiative.'

Many industrialists were, unsurprisingly, supporters of Taylor's work. Henry Ford the pioneer of mass production, was a huge fan, for example. Workers were often less keen. Fortunately for the general labour force, management theory began to move away from scientific management toward a more human oriented approach.

As early as the 1920s, Mary Parker Follett, an American political scientist was emphasizing the human element of management. She defined management as 'the art of getting things done through people.' 'Responsibility is the great developer of men', she wrote.

In a precursor to the human relations school of management thought of the 1940s and 50s, Australian psychologist, Elton Mayo, conducted a number of studies into motivation in the late 1920s and early 1930s. The Hawthorne Studies, as they were known, took place at Western Electric's Chicago plant. The finding revealed that teamwork and consideration of employees as individuals might boost productivity. Perhaps more importantly, though, Mayo began to shift attention from dehumanizing mass production to the need for humanity in the workplace. As Mayo noted: 'So long as commerce specializes in business methods which take no account of human nature and social motives, so long may we expect strikes and sabotage to be the ordinary accompaniment of industry.'

Since then, employees have gradually been afforded greater freedom to make their own decisions and contribute to the success of the organizations. The extent to which this has happened varies from country to country, organization to organization. In the 1970s, for example, Toyota motored ahead of competitors by incorporating management techniques such as continuous improvement as part of its Toyota Production System, empowering employees to contribute to the success of the enterprise. While more recently in the US, for example, at Google, the multinational internet related product and services firm, employees have 20 per cent time – allowing them to spend a proportion of their week working on their own ideas and projects, which may then became part of Google's business proposition.

There are sound commercial reasons for letting employees get involved in this way. Corporate history is full of examples of empowered employees making ground-breaking achievements for their organizations. At Google, for example, 20 per cent time produced innovations like Gmail and Google news.

At Microsoft under Bill Gates, for example, as the organization grew there was a conscious effort to use small empowered and autonomous teams to create a kind of start-up mentality. The point was to capture the energy and can-do attitude of a small business. 'Even if we are a big company, we cannot think like a big company or we are dead', Gates once said. The result was a campus of hundreds of employees clustered in small teams, but with a framework of rules that allowed for a high degree of coordination.

Contrast this with the way Nobel Prize winner William Shockley, possibly one of the world's worst managers, ran his team at Shockley Semiconductors, Palo Alto in the 1950s. Shockley was a brilliant scientist. His management skills, however, were less well developed. Among his more interesting management techniques, were lie detector tests he insisted his staff take, and the orders given to various project teams to keep the details of what they were working on a secret from their colleagues. When some of his employees expressed a desire to publish their own research papers, Shockley went off, wrote a paper, and offered to let them put their names on it. Shockley, it was noted, 'didn't have trust and faith in other individuals'.

If Shockley's management strategies were erratic, the results were more predictable. His most talented employees soon left en masse. Working elsewhere, these brilliant employees, the likes of Gordon Moore and Robert Noyce, helped create the silicon chip, and found CPU giant, Intel.

Drivers in Action: Autonomy and Empowerment

The Perils of Over-coaching

'One of the great challenges of coaching is over-coaching. When you want to empower people, they need to know they're playing on the pitch, what position they're in, and what the main priorities of the game are. But they also need to be allowed to demonstrate a bit of flair and creativity. So it's that kind of coaching – within reasonable boundaries, but never tying people down so they can't be creative and demonstrate flair.'

A senior executive in a large not-for-profit organization

Creating a culture for autonomy and empowerment

A culture which supports empowerment and autonomy does not just happen. At least not in most organizations. It needs to be carefully nurtured – the right ingredients, the right leadership, the right training and development. While the end goal is an admirable one, and may sound relatively easy to achieve, creating a sustainable culture in which people are empowered with the autonomy to thrive, and create additional value for their organizations, is a challenge. It is a challenge that many of the executives that we spoke to are grappling with.

Consider, for example, just one aspect of the empowerment picture. Fear of failure. One manager we spoke to told us a story which illustrates perfectly how fear of failure acts as a brake on discretionary effort.

The manager was staying with his wife at a five star hotel in Asia. Having returned to the hotel late in the evening, after a long working day, they ordered a glass of wine at the bar and then went to take it to their rooms.

'As we were getting into the lift we heard these footsteps behind us. A very nice lady from behind the bar said, "I'm closed now, I can't allow you to take that glass of wine with you." I said: "Okay, well first of all you just allowed us to buy it, and secondly we want to go up to our room."

'So then she got another glass, an identical glass, and said you can pour it into this one and take that glass with you. The reason for doing this was the glass. She was accountable for all the glasses behind the bar.

'She needed that glass back to make sure she had all her glasses. Because if she didn't she could be punished. So there was zero empowerment, and it led to a bizarre situation at a high end hotel.'

It may seem like a small thing, but multiply this type of behaviour and response across an organization and it is easy to see how a lack of autonomy can create situations that are damaging to the organization. Managers can do much to avoid these situations, providing that they pay attention to a number of areas.

Without fear

Organizations that want their people to go over and above the call of duty, should aim to create an environment where they feel safe to do so. If individuals are too scared to act outside of prescribed boundaries for fear of punishment, they are unlikely to contribute discretionary effort. At the same time, though, organizations cannot allow misdirected discretionary effort that damages the organization. The right balance has to be adopted to risk taking.

A manager outlined his approach to creating the right environment for autonomy to flourish without fear:

'A lot of this is about deliberately celebrating the people who are brave enough to take a risk on something. It's got to be a calibrated risk, you can't tell them not to fail, and, obviously, you praise them when that risk comes off. But what happens when these things don't come off is probably the most significant thing. You don't go witch hunting, or immediately holding enquiries.

'The attitude has to be, "it didn't work, this is where we are, how we going to build on this position." We find that this relaxes the people who are a bit fearful of having made a mistake. When they realize the leadership is less interested in the past, and more about how we get back out this hole we've created, you get incredibly positive response. Human nature expects a beating, when it doesn't happen you feel quite relieved, and then you do all you possibly can to recover it. It's so important to manage the downside of encouraging risk taking and if you get that straight then people are going to be with you.'

Coach, don't do

Many organizations claim to have a culture of empower-ment, where employees have a high level of freedom in the way that they work. Whether that claim stands up to the test in everyday business is largely down to the way people lead. No amount of written rules or policies will create a culture of empowerment. What is written down may play an important role, but ultimately it is the behaviour of managers and leaders that helps to bring the culture to life.

Leaders that understand and are able to create the conditions for autonomy and empowerment are needed at every level of the organization: from the front line dealing with consumers, to the senior executive team. This kind of leadership is not easy. Some individuals find it very difficult to manage others in a hands-off way.

'Autonomy and empowerment are very important', says Bar-oness Sue Campbell CBE, Chief Executive, Youth Sport Trust.

'Empowering someone means giving them the freedom to do it their way, not over-supervising them, but at the same time being there. It is a coaching style. The challenge is developing a management team and management style which embraces that consistently. Getting that coaching style right in your senior team to create that feeling of autonomy and empowerment. And then getting others to know how to coach that.'

The temptation to micromanage must be avoided at all levels. It is a common refrain from employees – they want to avoid being micromanaged. The kind of leadership that encourages autonomy, and discourages micromanagement, is rooted in the coaching and teaching tradition, rather than the showing and doing. 'It means moving away from a situation where things are over processed, and there are checks made of checks on checks, and then it is checked again by the CEO, for example. That's not necessary,' says Campbell.

'The challenges around this are first of all making sure that you're setting clear objectives, and checking in and guiding performance', says one manager in the leisure business. 'Then the key driver is that it is teaching people rather than doing it. Often what happens if you empower someone to do something and then they get it wrong is that the leader has the tendency to jump in and do it for them.

'So we have a really strong culture of wanting to teach. If someone does something wrong, instead of going back and saying, well that's not what I wanted on this PowerPoint, let me redo it, I will sit with them with the PowerPoint and say here's why it didn't meet my needs – so that they learn and do it better next time.'

Drivers in Action: Autonomy and Empowerment

Clear Objectives

'Trusting people to get things done is critical. But before that, you need to be clear about what it is you want them to get done, or what the company needs, what the effort required is.

'That may not mean telling them exactly what to do, but it means being clear about the end objective. It's a balancing act, because you want to be very clear about what you're expecting the end result to be, but you want to give them as much leeway to get it done as possible.

'That boundary setting will depend on the activity and role. If it is software development, for example, the organization may want them to be as innovative and creative as possible. If it is financial management, however, there may be certain rules and restrictions that help to form those boundaries.'

A senior executive in a global business services corporation

Freedom within frameworks

Empowering employees and allowing them independence can provide numerous benefits, but it also creates a number of challenges for organizations. In particular, many organizations may feel nervous about allowing individuals a high degree of autonomy because they fear that those individuals will behave inappropriately.

And it is true that there is the potential for individuals to cause considerable damage. After all, derivatives trader Nick

Leeson brought down Barings bank, the oldest merchant bank in London, established in 1762, by exercising his freedom by making trading decision in a way that did not benefit his employers. Working out of Singapore, Leeson managed to hide his losses for some time before fleeing to Malaysia, leaving a note saying he was sorry, and over £800m in losses. Similarly at Enron, the now defunct US energy giant, the errant actions of a minority of employees, including CEO Jeff Skilling and CFO Andrew Fastow, managed to capsize the entire company.

Yet it could be argued that there were more checks and systems to prevent aberrant behaviour in these organizations than in many others. If employees really want to behave badly they will find a way. Removing opportunities to exercise autonomy is not the answer. Creating the appropriate culture and frameworks to support and encourage the right behaviours by individuals is probably a better safeguard.

Employees who carry out instructions given to them by their manager, can usually assume that they are doing something that the company approves of. In a perfect organization, all employees would innately understand what was and wasn't permissible at all times, unsupervised or otherwise. But organizations are not perfect. If an organization wants to give its people the autonomy to make decisions on their own, it also needs to help them by providing some kind of framework to allow them to check that they are acting in an appropriate way.

There are several things that organizations can do. Much of it is about finding the right mix of control and freedom. 'You do need to find a balance', said one executive working in the financial services industry. 'You do that by putting in place a level of oversight. You have freedom within a framework. So within the framework you can pretty much do what you like, but outside the framework you need clearance or permission.'

Employees need to be aware of the boundaries that are set, and the organization needs to be satisfied that the employees understand. 'It comes down to communications and culture', says the executive. 'You make them very simple to communicate and understand.'

Drivers in Action: Autonomy and Empowerment

Taking Ownership

'So if I take the idea of "ownership" and what that actually means. One thing we're trying to do is to make sure that if I'm an adviser I deal with your problems from start to finish, that I don't get to the point where I think, I'll just transfer you to someone else. So to try and give a better customer experience, we're asking our advisers to really take ownership for their customers' issues, to really understand them. That involves asking the right questions, taking notes on what activities they're carrying out, and really trying to use all of their skills to resolve that. So in doing that, they have the autonomy to get on and solve a customer's problems as far as they can.'

A senior manager in a large multimedia business

Hiring, values and behaviours

Part of the boundary setting can be done during the on-boarding process, when the organization first hires someone.

This may be through documentation, some kind of induction process, the intranet, as well as through the complete mix of communications used in modern organizations these days. Although it is important not to make the message too complex and to avoid information overload.

Organizational culture, and in particular governing principles or values, play an important part in boundary setting, and enabling the construction of reference points as a guide to acceptable employee behaviour. Take the Red Cross, for example, its principles of humanity, impartiality, neutrality, independence, voluntary service, unity and universality, define the essence of what the Red Cross is about.

A Red Cross worker can be in the middle of a humanitarian crisis or a war zone, out of communication and having to make critical decisions on the ground. Although they may be unable to get guidance or permission for their intended actions from their managers, the Red Cross values provide invaluable guidance. No one who works for the organization is in any doubt about the parameters which instruct and inform their actions.

Many organizations have mission, vision and values statements. However, a lot of organizations fail to take the next necessary step of ensuring that the mission, vision and values are perfused throughout the organization and underpin the culture.

A good example of one organization with the right approach is the InterContinental Hotel Group. The hotel and leisure firm has created its five Winning Ways: Do the right thing; show we care; aim higher; celebrate difference; and work better together. These act as a touchstone for employees and have then been driven through the company.

"Over the past few years we've really undergone an effort to clearly define our values. These values are not just words on the wall, they are what we live by." One manager at IHS told me.

A lot of meaning can be packed into a few small phrases. As they went on to explain, 'aim higher' is about working better, smarter, and stronger. 'Work better together' is about collaboration. 'Celebrate difference' concerns the global nature of the organization, and the need to understand everyone's perspectives, whether that is regional, cultural nuances or even from a talent perspective. 'If you've got an IT person versus a business person, how do you make sure that you understand and leverage the strengths of each person? Someone may be more analytical, someone may be more of a big picture thinker, but you have to understand and leverage the talents of the individual person.'

'Show we care' is about making sure that the InterContinental people make a difference in the communities they work in (as well as the organization demonstrating that it cares for its employees and celebrates who they are).

And, finally, 'do the right thing' is about challenging the norm. 'So not just saying, hey, it's always been done that way so let's do it that way again.' 'It's really about let's challenge this if it's not the right way to do things or if there's a better way of doing things, or even if we have a difficult decision to make, right?'

Over the last few years the five winning ways have permeated through the culture of InterContinental Hotel Group, even to the point where it has become part of the organization's key performance objectives. So now people at IHG are not just measured on what they do, but also on those five competencies in terms of the way they act.

By outlining its Winning Ways and building these behaviours into its performance systems, InterContinental Hotel Group has created a strong organizational culture, and more particularly, terms of reference that employees can use to guide them in the use of discretionary effort. It helps to guide employee behaviours, while at the same time not micro managing them.

The value of values

Of course values must not be copied from other organizations. InterContinental Hotel Group's Winning Ways values, for example, are special to them. Other organizations will distil their own. These values must be authentic and meaningful, they must resonate with the organization and its people. Simple, fairly punchy, and short, are good guidelines to start with.

And then those values must be instilled and promoted within the organization. For the purposes of sustainability and ease of dissemination it can be an idea to capture the principles, values – or whatever name is given to them – in a lasting document. Johnson & Johnson, the pharmaceutical and medical devices giant, for example, has its Credo. Originally drafted in 1943 by Robert Wood Johnson, the chairman from 1932 to 1963, and a member of the company's founding family, the Credo contains the values that guide decision making in the organization – it provides 'a moral compass'.

At IBM, Thomas Watson Jr, IBM's CEO for 14 years, who began his tenure in the late 1950s, captured what the company stood for in his book, *A Business and Its Beliefs* (1963). Watson Jr argued that, to sustain the corporate culture required: 'a sound set of beliefs, on which it premises all its policies and actions. Next, I believe that the most important single factor in corporate success is faithful adherence to those beliefs . . . beliefs must always come before policies, practices, and goals. The latter must always be altered if they are seen to violate fundamental beliefs.'

In this case there were three basic beliefs underpinning IBM's business, established by Thomas Watson Sr, and continued by Thomas Watson Jr: give full consideration to the individual employee; spend a lot of time making customers happy; and – go the last mile to do things right. These beliefs served the organization well for many years. And, even though it may have lost its way, and almost the business, during the 1990s, Lou Gerstner was brought in as CEO steering them back on track, with a particular focus on doing things that make the customer happy.

Usually, there will be a significant education and communication drive implemented around the behaviours and values. The idea is to allow people to appreciate what the values are, and understand the framework within which they are able to operate, which then helps to regulate discretionary effort.

But it also pays to make sure that employees really do understand what kinds of behaviours are expected of them, and that they are acting accordingly. One of the more obvious ways of doing this, for example, is by gathering customer feedback.

'We try to get feedback from our customers from a variety of sources some directly, some indirectly, some independently, some from our own surveys. Some via telephone, some face-to-face, there's a variety of areas, just like there is a variety of transactions', explained one executive.

'You read complaint data – so why are people complaining? Is there an issue we have across the organization? Is there an issue with a specific team? Is there an issue with any specific individual or a type of customer? So it's really about sense checking from a variety of sources of data.'

One senior executive that we spoke to also engages in a spot of mystery shopping. While managers may be unable to conduct the mystery shopping in person – their well-known faces removing the 'mystery' element – there are still many ways of tackling this.

'You can do it by phone', says the executive. 'I do a variety of things. I ring up the same numbers as our customers ring up and I am treated no differently and I go through exactly the same processes and that's quite enlightening sometimes.'

Leaders at all levels, from front line managers to CEOs (especially CEOs) should be sampling the customer experience in a number of ways.

The power of empowerment

Depending on an employee's role, some organizations may be reluctant to empower individuals and allow them a high degree of autonomy. One common reason for this is that they do not believe that the employee's role is one that provides any scope for discretionary acts. A call centre worker, for example, may be given very limited scope to deal with consumer problems, or a retail assistant may not be entrusted with the power to help customers on certain matters. Thus the argument that the scope of a particular role means that there is no place for autonomy, empowerment, or discretionary effort is a comparatively common one.

Following my many conversations on the subject, however, I believe many organizations are simply being too cautious.

Obviously there are some situations that do not warrant an employee taking matters into their own hands. It would be wrong for a nurse to overrule a doctor's treatment decision, and choose to administer an alternative drug instead, for example. However, even in many situations where it seems as if the behaviour of an individual has to be highly prescribed, it is still often possible to provide employees with sufficient autonomy to make their own decisions, give discretionary effort, and create value for the organization.

A great example of what is possible, is the case of one company that makes extensive use of a paid-for software helpdesk as an integral part of its operations. If there are any problems with products, the firm provides a helpdesk service to its customers which they pay for. So, when the customer calls, it is invariably because they have a problem that needs dealing with.

As an executive working at the company explained, the long standing position was that an individual would be given a problem by a customer over the phone, and then pass that problem on to an appropriate person to deal with. It is a situation common with IT helpdesks, for example, where there is second and third line support, to maintain an adequate level of specialist knowledge. However, the effect of delegating problem ownership in this way was to de-skill the front-line workers, and consequently devalue the work, leading to a loss of motivation, and discretionary effort.

Still, the system appeared to work relatively well, and there was no strong incentive to change. The manager that we spoke to, however, believed that it was possible to create an even better working environment where the call centre employees could contribute much more value to the business.

'Like all good ideas it started with our people', the executive told us. 'We brought in a company to ask both our people and our customers what we needed to do differently around the technical support product that we deliver. The feedback that we got suggested that we needed to work on the whole environment – how we operated the structure, and how we empowered our people.'

The manager looked at the existing model, in terms of how it drove the people and how it measured them. As you might expect in a large centre, it was very much organized around productivity: how many calls; how long the call is; and then a customer satisfaction measure.

A decision was then made to remove the productivity measure, and focus on quality. At the same time there was a fundamental change in the way people dealt with problems.

'We allow our people to pick up the problem and see it through to fruition. The individuals manning the helpline are now empowered to keep hold of that particular interaction from start to finish, so they can go away, substantiate the problem, solve the problem, and then ring the customer back. That even extends to putting right what's wrong within the business that we needed to prevent the customer's problem the first time.

'They can get into the business and find out what the problem is, even to the point of feeding back to research and development, and saying you've got a bug, or we need to change something within the software in the future, in terms of capability. So we've really empowered them, by creating that environment where they can actually get a hold of something and move it forward.'

What is particularly interesting about this initiative is that there were disincentives for management to explore, trial and adopt the new system. Had the company approached the issue from a strictly cost basis perspective then they would not have implemented the changes because of the potential for increased costs associated with longer transaction times. Ostensibly then it is not a decision where a case can be made on a productivity basis, on the face of it. If anything, it is a decision that goes against the metrics. But, as the executive explained to us – they held their nerve – and although transactions do take longer, the propensity for the customer to contact the call centre for the same reason decreases.

And there are even greater benefits – although they took a little while to emerge. Initially the new approach was trialled for three months with three teams. When they first ran the trial it was, as the manager describes, 'absolute anarchy'. The staff were so used to their outlines that it was very difficult to get them to respond in a different way.

It was crucial that management made it clear that they were empowered and could make the decisions. That they would be supported, developed, coached and that the right conditions for them to succeed were being created. Staff were coached out of their engrained behaviours so that they could then adapt and develop the behaviours that they really needed. Within a couple of months the team saw a positive change as a result of this work, and the concept was taken to the regional board which sanctioned a wider roll out. Since then it has gone global within the company and been rolled out to 30 teams.

So, by actually empowering the employees to take true ownership of the problems the customers presented them with, the initiative provoked a behavioural change – the employees became more determined to deal with the issues.

'We've really seen people get a hold of things and give them a good shake, so that we can get things solved. Even to the point where we've had people go out and visit customers, which is not their role', said the manager. 'So our people have gone out there and done a face-to-face locally, and then what we've learned from that has been brought back into the business to improve the business and the support even further.'

So an environment has been created and the employees adapted to that environment. As a result the business began to see huge returns in the form of much better customer retention.

Drivers in Action: Autonomy and Empowerment

Do it Properly or not at All

As one executive explained, their organization ran an engagement survey for the top one hundred managers every quarter. All the way throughout this, there was one area that was much weaker. The area of weakness became apparent when they were asked: do you believe that everybody is treated with respect? They consistently scored below 50%.

Why? Because the organization was telling its people it wanted them to be more autonomous, yet at the same time exerting tight controls over them. So, for example, vacancies had to be signed off at CEO level, so if someone goes missing at a critical moment, managers can't just go and replace them – they needed three people to say that it's okay first.

It turned out that the feelings of lack of respect were tied to the areas where there were shortcomings with respect to autonomy. People felt that the organization was being disrespectful of their judgement because they were effectively insinuating that they didn't trust them to take sensible decisions.

Free to decide – Action Points

In trying to encourage autonomy and empowerment in organizations, you are likely to encounter the 'autonomy gap'. That is the gap between where you believe you should be with respect to these two behaviours, and where you actually are because of the reality that organizations are invariably rule bound and constrained by culture and KPIs.

Yet, while the ideal might be a situation where autonomy and empowerment is demonstrated by people acting wholly on their own for long periods of time and on large projects, these can also be introduced in small ways with, for example, people taking the initiative with a good idea for incremental improvements to business processes.

To create a culture in your team where autonomy and empowerment are encouraged, begin by changing the questions you ask around the team. Ask 'What can we learn?' not 'Who is to blame?'

People do not feel safe taking the initiative if they are afraid of the consequences; staff will only act in 'safe' ways if they fear for their reputation, job prospects or loss of privilege/rights. If, as a manager, you ask 'What can we learn?' when things do not go as planned, you create an environment whereby people know it is fine to try new things or step out of the normal ways of working.

Encouraging people to make decisions on their own and not punishing the results can begin progress towards autonomy and empowerment.

1. Run meetings with high inclusion and ownership
As a leader, if you solve all the problems, operate from a base of knowing all the answers, and run meetings in a directive

or autocratic way, you will have a passive workforce who will just wait to be told what to do. Alternatively, meetings run with high levels of inclusion and ownership of all team members present, mean shared responsibility and involvement in the running of everyday initiatives and business issues.

Meetings with high levels of ownership and inclusion will be obvious. They are likely to include:

- Discussion
- Debate
- Constructive disagreements
- Relatively equal involvement by all present
- Equal airtime
- Creative suggestions
- Humour
- Structure

2. Ask 'How do you like to be managed?'

And, crucially, act upon the response. Ask your team what support you can be to them, how they like to be managed, and what they need from you. It is easy to assume that people in your team are all similar to each other or indeed yourself. By doing this it will create the culture whereby the leaders and team members are able to operate optimally, not to be involved in a continual process of checks and balances.

3. Provide cover

As a leader, if you are going to encourage your team to act more autonomously you may experience criticism from higher up the chain of authority in your organization. Your role is to protect your team and this takes courage. If you truly believe your team is doing well and the empowerment will deliver results your role is to protect them from other organizational pressures. If they feel you are taking responsibility in this area they will be free to act upon their own authority and use their initiative without fear of retribution.

A good motto to lead by is 'take less than your fair share of the credit and more than your fair share of the blame.'

4. Expect things to be different

The final thing to consider when creating a culture based around this driver is to expect things to be different. More often than not, when you empower people, they will make decisions, create scenarios and solve issues in an entirely different way to you. You must expect and accept this. Focus less on how you would have done things differently, and more on how the overall cultural of empowerment positively impacts on the business.

4. GETTING TO KNOW YOU

'A little consideration, a little thought for others, makes all the difference.'

Winnie-the-Pooh

After one particular VP leadership event at a global bank, I got talking to one of the delegates. The conversation turned to disability and perceptions about disability both in general and within their business. Both of us could recall occasions where prejudice towards an individual meant that a firm missed out on the opportunity to employ a genuinely talented person, simply because of misguided beliefs about the impact of disability.

This led us to a further discussion about what constituted a disability within a commercial setting. I have always believed that disability should be viewed in the context of the task at hand. Agreeing with this view the VP suggested that, in the context of their business, a lack of empathy was a significant disability. Being an effective performer in a banking environment has a lot to do with the ability to build relationships. It was essential, that leaders were able to connect with other people and understand and appreciate them as individuals. And this is true for most business, not just in terms of the relationships with clients but also co-workers.

Unfortunately, in this particular business, for whatever reason, people that were technically good at their job but lacked this critical leadership quality were sometimes still promoted to leadership positions. And this is a common issue in organizations. Especially, for example, in organizations where length of tenure is still a key driver for promotion to a leadership role rather than people skills.

Treat people differently

The findings from the work by the research team at New York University suggest that getting to know and understand others, and what motivates and drives them, is a key factor in promoting discretionary effort. The term used to describe this knowledge and understanding of others is 'individualized consideration'.

The notion of individualized consideration was originally introduced as one of a number of elements involved in transformational leadership, a concept developed by James Mac-Gregor Burns, Pulitzer Prize winner, historian and leadership expert. Transformational leadership is about leaders and followers working together to improve individual morale, motivation and performance.

The more that you understand your people the more you are able to treat them as individuals in a way that elicits their best efforts. And the more likely they are to give discretionary effort.

Employees that feel valued are more likely to go the extra mile. And, in the case of individualized consideration, that sense of value arises because the other people they relate to in the course of their work – whether that is a leader, manager, peer, customer or other stakeholder – make them feel cherished, nurtured, and cared for. The individuals in the organization feel that their leaders and managers genuinely want to understand them. They want to know: what makes each employee tick? What motivates them? What are their values? What are they interested about outside of work?

As a leader of one organization said: 'I'd say knowing people beyond the job, is absolutely critical; I'd say that it is as important as empowerment.' While another said: 'If you don't understand your people, you're not going to understand what drives them. So we really encourage all of our managers to do that.'

The reality of the work today means that, in many modern organizations, demonstrating individualized consideration is becoming increasingly important. Teams are becoming more diverse. 'I try and recruit for diversity', said one manager, who is part of a large financial services group. 'What I mean by diversity is not so much around gender or cultural background, for example, which is still important, but more about how people operate, think and do things differently – creating more diversity of thought and ideas.'

Indeed, when diverse teams work well together, they are more effective than homogeneous teams. So, for example, work by Katherine Phillips (2009), a professor at Columbia Business School, New York, has shown that having 'strangers' as teammates can actually do more good than harm, leading to groups that produce better outcomes although they not may not recognize this in doing so.

Getting diverse teams to work well together is not always easy, though. For example, I believe that an increased emphasis on individualized consideration can help contribute to the social glue that allows diverse teams to work effectively together in general.

Good managers know their people well enough, to know which levers to pull and which to avoid in getting them to perform to their maximum. 'My team happens to be about ten people or so, and I definitely treat them all completely differently, because they've all got different characteristics', a manager of a global business service company, told me. 'So I know where the hot buttons are. I'm always thinking, "well, what do we want from this role within this team?" Then I'll try and adapt that to each individual's strengths and weaknesses, and interests and attitudes.'

How do I get to know my people?

So it is essential to recognize the importance of getting employees to feel that their boss, their team leader, their colleagues, care about what they really think, and want to understand what motivates them. But that is just the start. The challenge is making that happen. Creating an environment in which employees feel cared for and valued.

Some organizations are focusing considerable effort and resources on this particular driver of discretionary effort. Take one large communications company.

'We have been doing a lot of work with our management teams this year, on personal development and on management development, and a lot of this has been around the value of really getting under the skin of what's important to your individual team members, what makes them tick. What makes them feel that they have had a great day, or feel they've not had a great day', said one manager.

'Managers need to understand, for example, that people take the concept of how they're valued in very different ways. Some people will only feel that they've been shown that they're valued by having a big conversation about it, whereas for other people, all they need is a quick reference once in a while.'

This particular manager had done a lot of work with middle management, with the line managers and second line managers, working on the impact that they can have on their team as a leader, and understanding and valuing the differences within their team. 'It is partly about how you can grow an awareness of yourself, and an awareness of your team members, so that the overall outcome is a better understood relationship which has a better mutual benefit', they said.

Drivers in Action: Individualized Consideration

As one executive pointed out, there is no magic bullet. It is a mix of things: watching people in action; listening to the way they internalize what you said; asking them; it's probing; observing them. Use team meetings and offsites. You almost build a picture up through all of those different things. People may say that it is one particular thing that motivates them, but actually, when you observe them, you discover that it is something different.

Different strokes, for different folks

People have different attitudes towards sharing information about themselves. Some people are very open. Others, however, are far more private, unlikely to initiate a conversation, and certainly unlikely to tell you about their hopes and fears.

Both types of people represent something of a challenge for leaders and managers. With the more open person, the challenge is to manage the conversations so that they are time efficient, and also to be able to sift through the information and detect which is important and which is not. With the latter, the challenge is more about getting them to say something beyond the transactional, while making sure that they feel comfortable about that exchange.

As one manager said: 'You can tell fairly quickly what people are willing to share. Some people tell you everything, and more that you don't want to know. Other people are more reluctant. So it needs to be much more of an individualized approach in terms of how much the employee wants to share. You need to get to know them, to be able to trust them, engage them, figure out what excites them about the job.

'Then over a certain period of time you get to gauge if something is wrong. Whether or not it is the normal personal behaviour and output from the particular individual. Is there something going on? And I wouldn't hesitate to, very tactfully, ask those sorts of questions.'

And some persistence may be needed, noted another manager. 'I'm a bit relentless with trying to get inside people a little bit; getting beyond the superficial, and not being afraid to ask the questions that probe into and understand, those motivators, those drivers, why they did things. Some people allow you to do that more easily than others. But a key part of it is just being a bit relentless. Really asking the sort of probing questions, and also not being afraid to shut up and let silence play a role in getting people to open up.'

Organizations that pay attention to the concept of individualized consideration – although they may not recognize or use this phrase as such – will usually engage in a mix of activities designed to discover more about their employees. Some of these activities will be part of formally structured learning and development initiatives, while others will be informal activities, possibly outside of work.

Room to be yourself

A good example of what is possible is the 'Room to be yourself' programme run by the InterContinental Hotels Group. The company are keen to acknowledge the fact that everyone has unique interests and desires. People have a life where they enjoy doing things outside of work.

'We encourage them to fulfil those interests, and feel proud about them', said one executive at the firm. 'So we did a whole campaign called Room to be yourself. We actually did photo shoots of all our employees. We suggested that they came in to work, and showed us what they were passionate about, and then when they did we took pictures of them. So if they liked cooking, they wore their chef's hat, and brought along their pots and pans, for example.'

Go to the firm's website and you will see pictures of its employees doing what they love to do on their careers page. 'It's part of our culture. In fact, we encourage people to do this. Our website, particularly on the careers side, is very focused on this. Even in our elevator banks here there are pictures everywhere of all our employees, no matter where you go. It emphasizes that we love the fact that people are individuals, and that they have these passions, and that they really get into it and they talk about them.'

Targeted rewards

Another good way of expressing consideration for employees, and showing that you care about them is through the rewards and incentives that the organization offers. Most people have experienced those occasions when they get a sweater or pair of woolly socks, for Christmas – again. It is a nice gesture, but it is not really what you wanted, and not what you would have chosen had you been able to select the gift yourself.

It is the same with rewards and incentives. Rewards and incentives are far more appreciated by people if they are actually something that they like and, better still, want. Money is not necessarily the answer, either. Even though it allows the employee the chance to spend their reward how they wish. Awarding money, however, may not be the best method. If you are able to offer someone a reward tailored to that person it demonstrates how well you know and understand the individual concerned and it may be appreciated more. Or at least a choice between money and an alternative can be offered.

If a manager really knows their team well then they can personalize an individual's reward. Some people may like a bonus, some a fancy title, others may like half a day off to watch a child's sports day, while others are happy with a simple 'thank you'.

One manager explained how, after they had done a particularly good job, their boss gave them theatre tickets as a thank you. The impact of the gift was that much better than if it had simply been a sum of money, because the manager was a big fan of the theatre. So the reward matched his interest, and showed that his boss knew about his interests.

And it is not just what a person is rewarded with, either, but also the manner in which they are rewarded – as one manager acknowledged when he told us about the way that his organization tried to reward people.

'Obviously, we have to have the standard kind of rewards and measurements, but we do try to think carefully about what someone really likes to receive as acknowledgement for a good job. So some people love public attention. You know, they love to be brought up in front of a crowd and praised, and then some people hate that. And so we try to understand that before we do the praising', he says.

Walk the floors

It is difficult to understand what drives and motivates people if you do not get close to them. Walking the floor is one essential tool for leaders to help them get to know their people. Several people we spoke with emphasized the importance of getting out and about.

This manager's response was typical of many comments that we received on the subject. 'I walk the job, I know that is an old-fashioned thing to do, but I walk the job every single day I'm in. I'm in early usually, but once everybody's in, I'll go and make a cup of tea, and I'll just wander round, touch base with everybody, and I can sense what's going on in the building, I can sense if there's a problem', they said.

'And I'll sit down with a couple of people and say, how's so-and-so going? And what starts to happen then is that they automatically bring you things, and they'll talk to you. If I know what's going on in their lives sufficiently, then I can be there for them. Because I think that's when people feel valued – not just if you know what they're doing at the job, but more if you know the things that matter. People can't just leave those things at the door – they do bring them into work with them.'

Drivers in Action: Individualized Consideration

Reward in the Moment

'We don't switch off our care, it doesn't matter whether it's a board member or whether it is a member of the team, you keep that care about people.

'There is also a lot about showing appreciation, and in the right way. We've got an achievement scheme that rewards in the moment; you don't have to wait three weeks for it to go to a process. Someone can do a great job on one shift, and they will get a certificate and vouchers on the next.

Pass an internal audit, and you will get a call from the CEO or a board member, saying great job. Praise when it really matters.'

A senior executive in a major logistics firm

Different types of conversation

Much of what managers learn about the members of their teams will be through the conversations that they have with them, collectively and individually. These conversations are an essential part of the individualized consideration process.

Inevitably, there will be many thousands of exchanges with individuals over the course of a year, and the majority of these may well be of a cursory and functional nature. However, some of these conversations need to be of sufficient quality to at least find out more about what a person wants from their work.

There will be different types of conversation – some formal, some informal. In one organization, for example, there are at least four conversations that must take place between the managers and the members of their team, in order to discuss objectives. Those conversations have to cover setting objectives, discussing the development plan, a mid-year progress discussion, and then a conversation about how the manager can support the individual in moving forward with their development plan. How those conversations are scheduled is up to the manager.

Different people will need different types of conversation too. It may take some effort; however, leaders should learn to identify those employees that thrive on plenty of contact, while others require more attention to be motivated.

'If you really think about it, you should spend more time with the people who value your time more. Rather than with those people who are happy with just a quick check-in every now and again to motivate them, just a moment to say "brilliant job, well done,"' said one manager. 'So you need to understand what makes people tick. It is something that some people managers are great at it, do it fantastically, and that's what makes them fantastic at leading teams. But I don't think it is something that comes naturally to most people.'

The managers that are good at it, added the executive, are likely to come into the office on a Monday and ask team members what they did at the weekend. They will ask about the person's family and know the names of their children. They will talk about the person's objectives, how they see those objectives fitting into the overall plan, and how they feel about it.

Listening

It is not just skilful conversation that is an essential tool for managers intent on discovering what their employees want most from work (and life). Managers may do a lot of talking, but the best managers know when to keep quiet and just listen. Clever organizations ramp up the listening activity and roll it out across the workforce.

Retailers, and those organizations working with retailers or in the retail sector in some capacity, are often good at this. This is because their organization is set up to be highly sensitive to the needs of a particular constituency of stakeholders – the customer. Focus groups, surveys, tracking online consumer habits, understanding the psychology of the consumer – the best retailers have spent millions over the decades learning how to find out exactly what their customers want and need.

Perhaps it should come as no surprise, then, that they are often more easily able to direct some of these well-honed skills towards understanding their own employees a little better. As one executive from a well-known major retailer said: 'We spend a phenomenal amount of time out listening to colleagues. We've got one team that spends their life going out talking to colleagues. The CEO does it, all the board do it. The CEO has breakfast with a group of colleagues one Friday each month. We do listening groups all the time.

'If we are testing something we ring round the next day and see what our colleagues are saying, are they a bit concerned, are they happy, are they not bothered, so that we can always represent our colleagues. That's something that's really important for us. And so when we do our engagement survey each year we revamp it. We go out and we check that what we are measuring are things that are really important to our colleagues. Because what we might think is important sometimes, in our little world here, is completely different to what they are worried, concerned or excited about. So it's the only way to do it really.'

Of course, there are many ways for leaders to discover more about their staff members, and to allow teams to find out more about each other. It is up to organizations to find out which works best for them. There are plenty of examples of best practice out there to learn from.

Drivers in Action: Individualized Consideration

The Whole Picture

At a conference put on by one organization, a professional photographer came in and took a picture of all the senior people in one particular function. They were asked to divulge something that people would not necessarily know about them, and also why they loved working for their company. At the conference everyone played 'guess which description goes with which photo', and then afterwards the organization posted the headshots on its intranet complete with captions detailing their interesting facts.

Communication challenge

Individualized consideration may seem feasible enough to a leader with a small team. If a team consists of five people then you should be able to get to know them fairly well, although really getting to know them is still a bit of a challenge. But what if a team extends more widely? What about when you are dealing with large teams, or dispersed teams, or remote teams, or even an entire workforce? Then the communication piece becomes a little more challenging.

Visible leadership

Leaders can take the first steps towards meeting the communication challenge by making sure that they do not become hidden away from the people that they lead. They must avoid the stereotypical image of the CEO mogul, inhabiting a penthouse office in an eponymous skyscraper. Don't emulate Frank Winfield Woolworth, for example, who holed up on floor 24 of the Woolworth Building, the tallest skyscraper of its time, in an office that ran to 30 feet square, and was based on Napoleon's famous Empire Room, containing the clock and other articles from the original.

'Visibility is a key thing', said one executive. 'What ends up happening is that we get so busy in meetings or travel, especially as a global company, that a lot of times it can be a big challenge. If you're not seen or you don't walk the floor, people don't feel engaged with you as a leader, and may not understand what your motivations are. So we try to encourage that visibility.'

Other executives we spoke to echo those sentiments. 'I try and do visible leadership, the best I possibly can. So we don't go into an office and sit in a room in the corner, we go round and talk. That doesn't come naturally to a lot of people, so they have to practice it. But they get used to doing the role, if you like, in a way that isn't threatening, and in a way that increases the trust in the workforce.'

Drivers in Action: Individualized Consideration

'I'm really fortunate in having a CEO that really gets this. He's very keen on communicating; he's very keen on getting out and talking to people. I do a video of him every month. So we create a team briefing that goes out all about performance, the key messages, the vision, the values and generally how we're doing. There's always an introduction from the CEO with a PowerPoint presentation.

'But I also take him out to various sites and get someone to interview and film him. It's an opportunity to find out what's on employees' minds. Last month we were out at a grid site as part of the interview. It's a small office as well as the grid site. We got all the employees together and they asked questions. We then took three of the people and said, "okay ask your question to camera because this is your opportunity to say to the CEO what is on your mind."

'Once they have spoken to the CEO directly we then back this up with a round table session with 12 people, which will also include the executive team. The other thing we do is a dial in. So every month at least two or three of the directors, on different days, will be available to take calls and answer questions.

'We also have a thing called "through your eyes," which is basically a back to the floor programme. We send out a member of the executive to be with someone for half a day. They get to see what it is like to do their job. They don't go with any set agenda, it's just go there, meet so-and-so and do what they do.'

A manager from an energy company

At a distance

For people working in small, geographically proximate teams, the idea of getting to know team members may not seem such a daunting prospect. But while it is all very well getting to know a team of a few closely located colleagues, what if a manager is responsible for a more dispersed team? The good news is that it is still possible to take an interest in members of your team, even if they are based on the other side of the world.

When people are located in different countries, managers can master the art of idle chat when they are on a call, getting to know people a little bit that way, for example. Over time it is very possible to build a sufficiently strong relationship to both foster trust and inspire people to go the extra mile.

'I remember I had a guy who worked for me, one of my best employees', said a manager we spoke to. 'He managed a group of people himself. In the two years that he worked for me I never met him face to face. And yet, I trusted him to do anything and everything. I delegated a lot to him. Part of that was just spending a little bit of time with him on the phone, to get to know him, and talking to his previous managers. Just continuing to give him enough slack and watching the reaction carefully.'

In this case it was a very casual approach. Not a question of arranging a more formal, getting to know each other type conversation.

Not everyone finds it easy to have these types of conversation. But if you can, it is possible to use these conversations round the fringes of work to help you understand what people are like, and what drives and motivates them. Usually these are informal interactions. But there is also a place for more structured and formal interactions.

Cascading communications

Whether it is at a distance or not, if managers want to show large numbers of people that they care about them, the communication challenge is a lot tougher. To help get their message across, leaders can recruit others to help. First they must set a consistent example. They must get the leadership style and team right in the first place, and create the confidence that the leader's immediate team has the right ethos and approach to individualized consideration. Then the plan should be that this behaviour is reflected further down the organization. 'It's basically challenging those guys to do the same thing at the next level down', as one manager put it.

For example, at one organization, when there are situations which mean it is just not possible to assemble the entire team, they make a point of collecting together all those people with the responsibility for managing others. They do all-hands calls, so if there are more than 30 or so people on a line, for example, they use a managed conference bridge, where everyone is muted and press star one if they want to join to ask a question.

In this way, it is possible to maintain an intimate connection between managers and their teams all the way through the organization. At the heart of these types of cascading communications there still has to be the desire to find out more about the individuals managed and what motivates them.

One executive described it as being like a Russian doll. On the outside, the main part of the doll appears to be about where the company is heading. Peeling away the layers reveals different subsets. That might be the culture, it might be behaviours, and then a subset of that might be the annual deliverables for a department. But, when you get right down inside the doll, the fundamental core of it all is: What is it that motivates someone to achieve those things?

'It might be different things', said the executive. 'We have some people here, whose motivations are that they want to make people better, they want to be part of something, so you have to orient your discussions and the way you position things, in that context. Others are more commercially motivated. It's a matter of spending time with those individuals. So I have ten direct reports, who then have a similar number, so it really puts a lot of emphasis on leaders and managers to really get to know your people.'

Calling all people

Fortunately, modern communications make it much easier for leaders to reach large numbers of people – via a conference call, for example. One senior executive told us that just the night before we spoke to them they had spent 30 minutes on a call with 600 people, just to get an update on what's going on in their business. That is something that they did a least once a month, if not more often. The call is well publicized in advance. It is not mandatory; people dial in if they want to. And there is a question and answer session involved at some point during the proceedings.

It might not be everyone's idea of fun but, for the leaders who engage in this type of communication, it can be a highly effective way to connect with large numbers of employees and find out what is on their minds. 'If it's important to them then I need to know about it and get it sorted', says the executive.

Video conferencing is another possibility. One person we talked with had recently introduced Cisco's WebEx video conferencing technology as a pilot. That very morning, they had had a meeting with five people in one office at one city, two people in London, and various others dotted around the country. And, as most people have discovered, seeing someone when you talk to them can make a big difference to understanding meaning during conversations.

There are other methods, too, that are effective for communication with large groups of people. Some managers prefer to hold live, web-based question and answer sessions, whilst others hold all-hands town hall meetings.

At one point blogging was a popular way for senior executives to communicate with employees and the wider world. And many executives still maintain a blog, but it can be a substantial undertaking, as one manager noted. 'I do a blog, which I do myself and I update that every week. It's a double edged sword; because I thought it would be interesting and so I started it a couple of years ago, and it gets 1000 hits a week so I feel obliged to keep it going.'

For most managers, the methods of communication will be a mixture of the various options available: one-to-one conversations; management by wandering around; phone conversations, both personal and formal; conference calls; video conferencing; town hall meetings; and many others. Every individual has a preferred way of being communicated to. Some methods may be marginally more effective than others but the aim is to use a variety of means to engage with as many people as possible. Ultimately, the common threads that must run through all of these are a signal that the leader cares about the individuals they are communicating with, and that they see them as individuals, plus a degree of openness and transparency.

How much does your boss care?

It is surprising how many people remember bad managers from the past, who made little effort to find out about them as an individual. These managers really make an impression – the wrong one. Far more so, even, than the managers who did care. The message that came over loud and clear from the people we spoke to was that this stuff really matters.

'I can recall an instance where a manager obviously knew absolutely nothing about me, and made no effort to learn anything about me', said one manager. 'I was in a group meeting and somebody asked me a question about my children. The manager, who is on the phone, hears this, and asks, "now I've forgotten do you . . . you have kids, right?" This, after several years working for the particular person. I was shocked.'

It may only seem like a small thing to many people. However, this kind of management behaviour can have a profoundly negative effect on a person's desire to contribute to the organization over and above the contribution they are mandated to make. Regardless of how professional the employee's approach, they are unlikely to be motivated to go the extra mile.

'I didn't take it personally as much as I took it as a sign of very poor management and leadership. I'd have to say that I didn't go the extra mile for that individual. And whatever I did might have been for the greater good of the team, but not for this manager.'

Multiply the effects of that management employee exchange throughout the organization and it is easy to see what a devastating effect it can have.

As the same person noted: 'You're dealing with people, not machines. How you can maximize their experience and therefore their output without really understanding what makes them tick?'

Getting to know you – Action Points

As people we all want to feel significant – we all have a mind, a body, and opinions, thoughts and feelings which are very much our own and so we respond well when we are treated as individuals. It is crucial for leaders to recognize the importance of showing people in their team – and elsewhere – that they care about them as people. Not to let team members feel that they are just cogs in a large impersonal corporate machine.

A common saying is that we should treat people as we would like to be treated ourselves. This maxim, also known as the golden rule, or ethic of reciprocity, is a rich and ancient tradition featuring prominently in many religious and philosophical teachings. And for good reason. Because it is a great sentiment, and a perfect starting point for working with a team. The important thing is to then build upon this. Use this and your own beliefs and moral codes as a foundation, then hone your leadership skills by taking the time to get know your people. In practical terms a good leader will:

1. Be visible – MBWA (or management by walking about)
When a team member knows when and where he or she can find their leader they feel supported. They know their leader

is there should a need arise and they are more able to flag up issues and discuss problems before they become too onerous.

A good leader walks the floor at consistent times. If you cannot be there in person because you manage a remote team then use all the other forms of being present that are available in the modern world. Phone, text and Skype all work well if used judiciously and constructively. Weekly catch-up calls and texts at crucial times go a long way to supporting remote teams. Combined with planned visits in person, leaders and team members can create strong bonds of trust and support.

And remember, visibility should not just be physical, you need to be emotionally visible too. It is no good expecting people to tell you about themselves if you are not willing to give up information about your own life. A great place to start is when you notice something you have in common – children's ages, sporting interests, holidays in similar destinations.

2. Build a personal database – be interested, not interesting

Collect information, hoard details about your team and use and respond to them with interest and compassion. Teams thrive on a balance between task cohesion and social cohesion. Often the task cohesion is strong due to deadlines and metrics. However, the social cohesion is just as important for teams to be sustainable in the long term. By collecting information on your team you strengthen the bonds which tie you. Simple data such as:

- Birthdays
- Family members names and jobs or school stages
- Interests, hobbies, sports and pastimes
- Previous experience

Outlook and all mobile phone address books now have spaces for notes about your contacts. By collecting these you will be able to refer back to them. A mention of a team member's child's birthday or move to senior school demonstrates how a leader values that individual.

3. Ask advice

This is an excellent way to bring a team member closer, especially someone who feels alienated from you or the team. It is a good way to build bridges if there has been a difference of opinion, and to reconnect with someone after a cross word. People immediately feel valued if you ask their advice, opinion or suggestion they may have for improvement. Not only that, but you might get some great new insight. Leaders do not always need to know the answers but they do need to know where to go to get them. Asking advice and getting a good result can strengthen your relationships but also your position as a leader.

4. Do it because you care

Remember, though, individualized consideration must come from the heart. You do it because you care about your colleagues, not because you know you ought to. Authenticity is essential. Otherwise you will just appear fake and not genuinely interested, and this can be almost as damaging as not bothering in the first place.

5.   PUTTING OTHERS FIRST

'In this world it is not what we take up, but what we give up, that makes us rich.'

Henry Ward Beecher

For several years I have worked with P&G, the global manufacturing giant and, during a social event, I got talking to an employee who was telling me how much they liked and admired their leader. I asked if they could give me an instance or example of the leader's behaviour that made them feel this way and, interestingly, it wasn't the typical attribute or competency that I was expecting.

The business had been through an exercise where a series of 360 degree type reviews and feedback sessions had been conducted.

What impressed the P&G employee was that their team leader had shared their feedback, both good and bad, with the team. They were in no way obliged to do so, but felt that by demonstrating that they were willing to share their strengths and weaknesses, they would encourage a more open dialogue about the team's capabilities. At the time the team was working through a change programme and this leader was leading by example, placing themselves in a potentially uncomfortable position for the greater good of the team.

To take another example, a CEO of a large company went to visit one of the regional offices one evening. While he was there he came across an employee who was finishing off some additional work to make sure a particular task was completed. However, as a result of staying late, he was going to miss his bus ride home. The CEO, recognizing his discretionary effort, offered to give the employee a lift home, even though it was well out of the CEO's way.

These are examples of self-sacrificial leadership, where a leader demonstrably acts in the interests of others, including the organization, rather than in their own interests. In turn this inspires others to provide discretionary effort.

As one manager of a huge multinational firm said: 'Almost in principle, I have a problem with the leader taking actions that aren't in the interests of the common cause. As a leader, my personal interests have to be completely aligned with the interests of the organization, the department I lead, and the people that are in it. It's just non-negotiable. As soon as there's a divergence, there's a big problem.'

Unfortunately, most people will have seen a boss, manager, or team colleague, acting in a way that feathers their own nest rather than benefits the organization they work for. Focused on pursuing personal interests and advancing their own career, the decisions that they were making were not organizationally driven, in the first instance. They were personally driven.

'That's a recipe for failure for that individual', said one manager. 'As a leader, all of those things have to be pointing in the same direction. If there's any divergence, while it might work in the short term it will all come to a sticky end. People will either leave, or the person will be fired, or the performance of the group will take a huge hit.'

Creating a culture of service

An organization, then, needs to create an overall culture where the ethos is that people are there to serve others, whether that is serving external or internal customers, and that includes the most senior leadership, every level of management, and every employee. The idea of service should permeate throughout the organization. It should eventually become second nature for employees and, as with most aspects of corporate culture, the tone will be set at the very top. The behaviour of senior leaders will make the rest of the organization feel comfortable about putting the needs of others before their own.

As one manager said: 'We work to one maxim within the leadership team; it's that we work for our people, they don't work for us. So if they're not succeeding, that's because we're not doing something, not that they're not doing something, and that's a philosophy change that's taken me about two years to get through.'

The idea of taking responsibility for your actions must flow through the organization. It is a concept that I became very familiar with as a swimmer. Lars Humer, Olympic and Paralympic Swimming Coach (and my swimming coach for some time), has a coaching philosophy founded on personal sacrifice and taking responsibility. 'If the behaviour doesn't change it is the communication that has been unsuccessful', he says talking about his coaching role. If he failed to achieve change he would never place the blame elsewhere. Instead he would consider that it was his fault for failing to communicate why it was so important to change.

As difficult as it may be to coach and lead like this, putting your own reputation in the firing line along with your line manager, gets more people on board and maximizes the team's discretionary effort.

Selecting employees with the right characteristics

Sacrificial leadership implies that leaders take conscious actions that are primarily in the interest of others rather than themselves. They make a conscious choice not to put themselves first. Ideally, such actions would be subconscious and instinctive. While this is probably not the case for all leaders at all levels, organizations can make progress towards creating a culture of service, starting with the hiring of employees with the right type of characteristics. When you hire and promote, when you move people through the talent network, it pays to select those people who evidence those kinds of behaviours in the first instance.

As one manager put it: 'You've got to go for the sort of people that naturally, without being asked to do it, want to see other people doing well. Their job is about supporting other people to do well, rather than telling people what to do.

'If you are going to successfully foster an environment where discretionary effort isn't seen as an extra chore, and is actually something that people do naturally, you've got to be like that yourself, and you've got to be looking for that in your own senior management.'

That is all very well, but how do you determine whether someone has those qualities or not?

Drivers in Action: Sacrificial Leadership

Selfless Culture

'The biggest way I can advance my career is not to stand up and say "here is what I've done," but if others say, "you know what, he worked really well with me on that project. He was a team player, very engaged and carried me with him towards our goal." That does more for my career. It is really more about what have we done as a team. It is of more value that you are able to engage your stakeholders and make other people engaged in what you're doing.'

A senior executive in a major multinational
operating in the leisure industry

New hires

It is not always easy to unearth self-sacrificial leaders when recruiting from outside the organization. When a culture of service is well established, and the chain of command, and talent management process is consistently looking for this type of person, the process is easier. However, the challenge is that in many organizations, where this culture is not prevalent, these people are hidden away quietly doing their work supporting others, and not out there engaging in career enhancing self-promotion – and thus highly visible to external recruiters.

However, it is possible to evaluate these characteristics when assessing an external candidate during the recruitment process. The way to do it is to delve deeper into personality and leadership style, and the way the individual has accomplished projects and team and organizational objectives, and not just to focus on technical competence. Beyond checking on technical skills and qualifications, head-hunters will interview individuals asking them to relate detailed examples of the types of activities they have been involved in.

They will also interview referees in some detail, asking about their leadership style. Some will make a point of talking to people where their working relationship with the candidate has not been entirely smooth.

As one manager indicated, a significant indicator of a person's leadership style that is relevant to the issue of self-sacrificial leadership is the extent to which they use the words 'I' or 'me' when talking about their achievements. The person the organization should be looking to hire is the person who is clearly proud of the fact that they have helped maybe 50 or 100 people, or a smaller team of 10, perform well in the past. For this particular manager, so long as the technical competences were ticked, they would always go for the sort of individual who describes his or her past success by reference to the team that they have helped to be part of that success.

Career reassurance

Culture

Another barrier to cultivating self-sacrificial leadership behaviours is the career advancement processes and informal
promotion networks that operate in many organizations.

Leaders may well feel that if they want to be promoted then
they have to be visible to the senior decision makers in the
organizations. They may feel that if they act in a self-sacrificial
manner, and behave in ways that benefit the organization,
but are not necessarily in their own interests, then their
promotion prospects will suffer. They may, for example, assist
their team in meeting targets, but in doing so get behind with
their own work. And, therefore, this kind of self-sacrificial
behaviour is politically a mistake.

They may feel that is not enough, certainly in terms of ensuring career progression, to work quietly with others towards
achieving organizational goals, and that their success in doing
so will inevitably be recognized and they will be promoted
as a result.

Instead they may believe, as many managers do, that it is
necessary to be seen to be succeeding – to be visibly successful. They may feel that others will benefit if they share the
credit for success, and so they should claim responsibility,
even if that doesn't reflect the reality of the situation, where
they were not actually the sole person responsible.

The way to deal with this challenge is through organizational
culture. Throughout the organization, throughout the human
resources system, it must be made very clear that when you
behave in a self-sacrificial way you actually do get ahead with
your career. You can still be promoted if you are talented

enough. While, if you behave only in your own interests, you certainly won't get on.

All in it to win it

Another thing that organizations can do to promote self-sacrificial leadership behaviours is to incentivize these kinds of behaviours in people. Incentives in organizations are often targeted at individuals, through the likes of individual re-cognition and awards, non-monetary rewards, or financial incentives.

However, sacrificial leadership organizations will benefit from moving to assessment and reward systems that are based on team performance, rather than those based mostly on individual performance or technical excellence as a leader.

'The greatest accolade a manager or a leader can receive is for their team to win something, and to be recognized', said one executive we spoke to. 'The pride that goes through that team, but also the manager, in those instances is incredibly valuable.'

The executive points to the example of their recent team-of-the-year awards: 'It was closely contested, fiercely fought over, and had an amazingly positive effect on the engagement of the people involved. The leader has gone up many stages in the rankings, and he's more proud and happier about the team achieving something, than he would be if you picked him out and said, "hey, you're manager of the year, that's for sure."'

There need to be some metrics around measuring an indi-vidual's performance in the context of the team performance, or the broader performance of the organization. Whether that is as a productive member of the team with a view to future leadership, or as an existing leader of a team. Then it is question of seeking out those individuals that exemplify the desired attributes and behaviours, and making sure that they are part of the talent pipeline.

'We assess people now more by how well the team is motivated, how well the team is performing', said one manager in a large service firm. 'The results tend to be driven by the team, if there's a great leader on top who's providing great guidance then that is fantastic. The real skill in leaders that we're looking for, though, is somebody that gets his people excited, enjoying things, creative, displaying the right sorts of collective oriented behaviour.

'You can have a genius leading a team, but it doesn't work because that genius doesn't have the sort of style of leadership which fosters teamwork and buy-in. We know our best leaders are the ones where their teams display high levels of energy and enthusiasm. Usually that type of leader doesn't grab the limelight and is very happy to sit back and let the team do the talking.'

Still room for cash

It is worth noting that some managers stressed to us that there is still a place for pure cash for performance. It allows management to measure performance accurately. Rather than use it for individuals, though, it should be used on a team basis. Explain to everyone in the team what the targets are and, just as importantly, that if they work together they have a much better chance of achieving their target.

So if, for example, a team is pursuing a numerical target – say, volume of sales, or net amount sold – the team will also be in line for a collective financial reward for achieving this target. And, as an essential aspect of the financial incentive, everyone will get the same if they achieve the overall goal. This emphasizes placing team gain above individual glory.

Other aspects of assessment

There are other ways for organizations to assess self-sacrificial leaders and their individual contribution to the team, other than team performance *per se*. This is significant, as team performance doesn't give the whole picture.

It is important, for example, to cross check performance across the business stakeholders that an individual interacts with on a regular basis. Invariably people will interact with a range of people, both inside and outside the organization, often outside the natural borders of their day-to-day remit. Evidence from these types of interaction should be gathered on a regular basis. And so, while the direct line managers will be delivering performance assessments, much of the information they provide will be channelled from, and cross checked with, other sources across the organization.

'If I'm writing a performance review for one of my people', says one manager, 'I would reach out to their key partners and ask how they thought that person had done. I would go to whoever their customers are – for my team that is internal customers, but it might be outside the organization to your customers and suppliers and other stakeholders in the network.'

The 360 degree review is a standard tool in these types of performance assessments and can be used very effectively in various modified forms.

Another useful tool is the engagement survey. These anonymous surveys usually provide a picture of how different areas of the company are performing with respect to employee engagement.

'Results are almost always better where there's a good manager leading a business. And, with the engagement scores, you see improvements, comments, and trends in those scores, which support the fact that the management is strong. I've never really encountered a situation where I've seen a manager who's a great leader, with great motivation in his team, who is causing problems in another way.'

A high degree of trust in the culture of the organization is required. It would be easy for employees to think that if they are not highly visible in terms of achievement, if they are not claiming credit for themselves, then they may get passed over for promotion. Especially if this is their experience of how career advancement has worked in previous organizations or in the past within their current organization. So they really have got to trust the culture of the organization.

'It has to come from right at the top of the organization, and people have to feel secure that it is not going to change next month, or next year, as well.'

As some of the executives we spoke with also noted, a rapid turnover of personnel with leaders and team composition changing very frequently can create an additional barrier to creating a culture where sacrificial leadership can flourish.

A degree of stability is required. It allows individuals to develop the confidence that will allow them to focus on getting their people to perform better, rather than putting themselves in the limelight. When leaders change, however, it encourages people to consider adopting a different stance, and raising their profile, putting themselves forward to attract the attention of the new leader. It is 'a natural human reaction', according to at least one manager we spoke to.

Not just what you do – but how you do it

It almost goes without saying that success, and thus performance, should not only be measured by what a person has done over a period of time. Equally important is the *way* that they have performed, and the *behaviour* they have exhibited.

As one person we spoke to put it: 'it's so engrained in our culture that if someone achieves something, but they leave tons of bodies in their path, they're not considered successful.'

Personal leadership behaviours

Self-sacrificial leadership is partly down to the leader and the way that they behave. It is important to remember, too, that it doesn't have to be some enormous act, some sweeping grandiose gesture. Small actions can be hugely effective so long as they mean something to other people.

After you

As is often the case in organizations, senior leaders set the tone for the rest of the organization across a range of behaviours and activities. With respect to self-sacrificial leadership this means senior leaders should visibly promote behaviour that demonstrates that they place the needs of the organization and others ahead of their own needs.

As mentioned previously, the simplest of acts can make an enormous difference in terms of signalling the right kinds of behaviour. For example, you may have dozens of items on your to-do list. And everyone will know that you are busy and have a lot on your agenda. But, when a team member needs help, or the team as whole needs help, then as a sacrificial leader you will put your priorities for the day to one side, roll up your sleeves and get stuck in with the team to get them over that particular difficulty. You sacrifice what you need to do to help them for the better of the organization.

One executive who worked in a customer services unit of a large media organization offered their perspective, describing customer facing situations when they expect to see sacrificial leadership in action. So, for example, if there are too many customers in a queue, and people know generally that there are customers waiting, they would expect higher levels of activity – people jumping to things a bit quicker than usual.

What they would not want to see is a lot of managers all sitting behind their desks – this does not give any sense of urgency or any sense that there needs to be a behavioural change in similar situations. The managers should be sending the message that for the next half hour, or hour, or whatever it takes to reduce the queues, people are going to put the needs of the customer and the organization's mission to service customers above their own.

So the managers should be putting down whatever they are doing at the time, and encouraging their teams, helping answer queries, helping to take calls. That may well go against what they had planned to be doing for that hour, but once in a while it helps in terms of giving the team something to show that 'we're all in this together'.

It is a great example, because we all have our own to-do lists, things that we absolutely must get done. We all know how important it is to us personally, because if we don't get through doing these things it causes personal pain and aggravation. And we all know how frustrating it is not to be able to get on with those things we need to do because of interruptions. So, when a leader puts aside what they are doing, in order to help other team members and the interest of the group as a whole, and clearly not for personal gain, that is something we should all be able to appreciate and learn from.

The leader as coach and mentor

Another way that individuals fulfil their role as a self-sacrificial leader is through coaching and mentoring others. A good mentor enters into a relationship expecting nothing other than commitment from their mentee. And a good coach is focused on the improvement in performance for the people that they support. Sharing knowledge and insight with no obvious return can be infectious within an organization and can lay the foundation for a supportive and caring culture.

Leaders should not only make an effort to coach and mentor others, but be coached and mentored as well. The further up the hierarchy a leader rises, the harder it can be for them to find appropriate learning development opportunities. As one person put it, 'The problem you have got when you are at the top, is that there is not much above to help you, but an awful lot alongside you.' Nevertheless, many of the best leaders have a coach or mentor – or several – although it may not be a formal relationship.

When you are at the top it can be difficult to find people who are willing to tell you 'unpleasant truths'. Tales of people sucking up to the boss and telling them exactly what they want to hear are common. But this is unhealthy and risks creating leaders who think that they can do no wrong.

Coaching and mentoring can help avoid this. So, in one example, a very senior executive explained how they used a colleague in their organization as an informal mentor and sounding board, simply because this person would provide an honest and straightforward opinion; even though that person wasn't aware that they were fulfilling that function. In addition, the executive had two people outside the organization, who performed a similar function.

Staying in touch with who you are

To be effective, leaders must be authentic. There is nothing new in this, and it is an often touted fundamental of good leadership. It is worth mentioning, however, both because of its importance to sacrificial leadership and also because it is a tenet of leadership that often goes unheeded.

Authenticity is an essential aspect of self-sacrificial leadership. The desire to serve others must be genuine. Also essential, however, is a different aspect of authenticity. Leaders should try to retain a sense of who they were when they started out on their leadership journey. They must not allow leadership to corrupt their ideals, or to engage in leadership and a rise to positions of power and responsibility just for the sake of power itself.

Hubris is defined in the dictionary as excessive pride or self-confidence – some might say arrogance. It has long been recognized as a serious character flaw in leaders. In Ancient Greece hubris was a crime. There is no place for hubris in sacrificial leadership. There is no room for self-importance.

If anyone understands the concept of serving others you might expect it would be individuals working in a non-profit, serving the interests of a section of the community rather than those of shareholders. Even here, though, the savvy leaders are aware of the need to stay grounded.

As Baroness Sue Campbell CBE, chair of Youth Sport Trust put it: 'I think where the challenge comes is as you begin to promote people, as you begin to give people "power." Sometimes that power, as we all know, is intoxicating, and they start to almost fall in love with the power, rather than with the mission.

'It's somewhat easier [to avoid] in an organization where you're clearly on a mission that is about changing people's lives. I can't stand up in front of groups of people and advocate that I believe sport has the power to change lives, it has the power to help kids behave better, it has the power to help kids grow and develop self-esteem and then, at the same time, be saying that I'm the most important person here. So I think it's much easier on a charitable mission to live out this business where you're primarily working in the interests of others rather than yourself.'

Campbell is well aware of the need to stay grounded as a leader. 'I think you have to always remind yourself how insignificant you are in the order of things', she says.

A lack of hubris is certainly not a quality that should be confined to leaders in non-profits. It is just as important to avoid for leaders in all organizations, large and small, public and private.

It is easy to schedule activities to keep leaders in an organization grounded. In Campbell's case, among the many other things she does each year, she takes part in Easter Camp for kids. The event is held in Loughborough in the UK, and the kids, many of them from deprived areas, come from all over the country to attend.

'You need to be grounded. To get back on the shop floor and realize what it's really all about. I try every year to do this camp with these kids', she says. 'For four to five days, I won't take any other appointment, I live with the kids, work with the kids, deal with the problems that come and go. I spend the morning with them on their own, just me and them for an hour each day. And then at least once or twice a month, I do something close to the grass roots. It might be to go and open a local cricket club, for example, or something similar. Something, somewhere, where it reminds me, day-in and day-out, what it takes to make things happen.'

Showing everyone that you love what you do

Employees look to their leaders to model the right behaviours. That is what the best leaders do. That includes putting the needs of others before your own. Perceptions matter.

One person we interviewed told us how they viewed the CEO of their division. This person had risen through operational roles until they finally reached the top spot. 'You look at him and you have that distinct feeling that he's doing what he believes is right for the company', they said. 'He doesn't talk about money, he doesn't talk about self. You don't hear him saying he's got five or six cars at home. He talks about the products, about how proud he is of the company.

'If you see any leaders talking about how they love their work, and how they want to take things to the next level, and want to see improvement, and you get a sense of genuineness from them, then you automatically get people that want to follow you.'

Passion and pride are contagious. When leaders demonstrate how passionate they are about their work and their organization, it inspires other employees. Many leaders avoid discussing emotions. Or at least they are reluctant to talk about positive emotions like love, but often not so reticent to display anger or displeasure.

Kevin Roberts, CEO Worldwide of Saatchi & Saatchi is a good example of an inspirational CEO who is not afraid to talk about emotions in the workplace. He created the concept of Lovemarks and spread the message in his book *Lovemarks: the Future Beyond Brands*.

When he talks about his role he talks in terms of what he can do for his organization and his people. He talks about being the 'brand manager of Saatchi & Saatchi, responsible for sustaining the enterprise and the brand, the brand equity that the people have worked so hard to create over the past 40 years. And then the head of talent making Saatchi & Saatchi a magnet for talent. Because if we get the best people, we win.'

How does he get the best talent? By offering people: responsibility; learning; recognition; and *joy*. As he explains: 'I get the most joy when a great idea from Saatchi & Saatchi makes a difference in culture or society. And there have been a few.

Putting others first – Action Points

Putting others first does not always come naturally. Understandably, as individuals, we are concerned about our own career progress, our own work, our own lives. We worry about how others view us, and whether we make a good impression.

At its worst, self-interest can dominate the way some people operate at work. Managers trample over their team members and other managers as they scramble for pole position in the race for promotion. They claim responsibility for the success of others, and may even bend the rules and behave unethically to achieve objectives and goals. This is the antithesis of sacrificial leadership.

Both collaboration and cooperation are increasingly important in the way that organizations achieve competitive advantage and meet their targets. Organizations get things done by great teams working together. For this to happen, people must frequently put the interests of others – their organization, business units, team members, team leaders, colleagues, customers – before their own. And it is the leaders in the organization that will need to set an example in doing so.

Setting the right example takes time. Farmer's decide what crops to plant, prepare the land, sow the seeds, nurture the young shoots, feed the crops with water and nutrients, and only then reap a good harvest. We need to apply similar diligence and consideration to our relationships. Consistent behaviour over time makes the most difference.

1. Be accountable – keep promises and admit mistakes
Your team would prefer it if you didn't promise to do something at all, rather than promise to do something and then fail to deliver. It is one of the cornerstones of leadership behaviour and, in fact, customer service. If you make a promise or a commitment or even suggest you will do something then follow it through. Inconsistency and unreliability damage relationships.

Owning up to errors and mistakes is part of this. 'A good leader takes more than their fair share of the blame and gives more than their share of the credit', said American humourist, Arnold Glasow.

2. Mentor and coach

Mentoring and coaching others within your organization not only ensures that you are developing the individuals concerned but that you are developing the capability of the business as a whole. Equally as important, though, is that by entering into such relationship your knowledge and beliefs about the business filter through. People get a better sense of what matters to you and can see your passion for what the business does and how it goes about it. Above all it shows that, when necessary, you are willing to take time out to put the learning and development of the people around you before your own.

3. Don't gossip – avoid talking about co-workers, line managers, customers or the company when they are not present

Tempting as it is, this is one quick way to show a lack of personal integrity. Talking about people who are not present can be amusing, and colluding in the moment may offer a frisson of excitement at being 'in the loop'. However, how would you feel if you knew that other people were gossiping about you behind your back?

This gossip extends to the boss, the company and in fact all levels of the organization. As a leader you should be able to operate in such a way that this kind of destructive conversation is not necessary. This can be even worse when it is about company policy or decisions made by the senior leaders. If you do it you automatically create an environment where this type of behaviour becomes acceptable and this undermines confidence in you, the leaders and the whole company.

You can still have fun and be light-hearted; the question is whose expense is it at?

4. Notice your own shadow

You may be feeling the pressure, work issues may be bearing down on you. But if you are a leader, you must be careful how any anxieties, concerns and worries that you may have affect others.

Your team will gauge how you are feeling and adjust its feelings accordingly, especially in tough times. If you walk into the office with a stressed appearance, a frown and irritable responses, they will assume all is not good with the world and with them or their future.

The shadow you cast is spread wider than you think. Be aware of it, how you behave, how you respond to challenge and crisis, how you walk into the office in the morning will all impact on the team and if they don't know the reasons for your mood they will make it up and fill in the gaps, often with a negative spin.

A frantic, edgy leader creates a team in the same mould. Notice your shadow; be aware of how you respond in meetings and in front of colleagues.

5. Work with truth not perception – be transparent, talk straight

Be clear, honest, seek the truth, clarify expectations and think more about what is right than your own self-image and interests. Leaders with a reputation for telling the truth, and acting in a transparent way, get more support and trust. People like to be led by people they know they will get a straight answer from. The corporate world can be a place of hidden agendas, mixed messages and image management. Avoid becoming known as a person who is associated with these things. Otherwise people will assume you are acting on a persona agenda.

So, speak the truth and seek it in others, give honest feedback when asked, and step up and say what needs to be said. All this can be done with sensitivity. There is no need to be rude and aggressive with it. The simple rule, 'Tough on standards and kind to the people', works well in this instance.

6. Be the best self you can be

The usual message is that leaders must be authentic and true to themselves. And, on the whole, that is good advice. However, that does not mean embracing unhelpful personal characteristics that are likely to impair your ability to lead, just because they are a part of your make up.

Leaders that feel the temptation to put their own interests before those of their team and organization must try and temper that temptation. Instead, certainly if they want to create an environment in which their employees are more likely to give extra effort, they must try their best to be a sacrificial leader.

The pharmaceutical giant Bayer produces a vitamin product called Berocca. The marketing information on their website describes it as 'a unique combination of B vitamins, vitamin C and essential minerals which can help release energy and may help support concentration and alertness.' Their strap line is: 'You, but on a really good day'. Our research project didn't stretch to the point of seeing if vitamin supplements improved leadership abilities but the strap line is something you should be aiming for. So do try to be yourself. You, but on a really good day.

6. FAIR'S FAIR

'In our hearts and in our laws, we must treat all our people with fairness and dignity.'

Bill Clinton

In business, competition is considered highly desirable, indeed necessary for the optimal functioning of markets and the economy. So much so, that many organizations have imported competition as an ethos into their organization. Employees compete against each other in various aspects of the business, pitting business unit against business unit, team against team. The competitive ethos engrained in some organizations runs all the way down to setting employee against employee. There are companies, for example, that rank employees on performance with a fixed percentage at the bottom discarded on a regular basis.

However, while a climate of competition inside an organization may bring some benefits, if not managed carefully it can also create a culture and environment that discourages discretionary effort, and negatively impacts on the performance of the organization. Especially if it leads employees to feel that they are being unfairly dealt with.

One of my clients, for example, prides itself on generating internal competition. For some time now it has rewarded employees based on how they perform compared to their contemporaries, rather than measuring and rewarding performance against a specified goal or objective.

Unfortunately this model means that you can perform exceptionally well but still be at the bottom of the ranking system and therefore the reward system. An employee's job might be to sell 100 widgets per year. Over 12 months they might sell 110 widgets. On the face of it a commendable performance and one they should feel pleased about. However, if the rest of the team sells 120 widgets each, that employee would be the worst performer in the team and rewarded as such. In my client's organization a significant proportion of the employees feel the system is unfair. And, as we will see, this perception of unfairness has a significant impact on performance and, in particular, any desire to contribute additional effort.

Some people, as the company in question may well do, take the attitude that if it gets the job done, and the business is performing adequately, then why worry. But what if you worked in an organization like that? Would you share information with your team, for the benefit of the team and the organization, or keep it to yourself? Put yourself in the widget salesman's shoes. Would you work for yourself, trying to figure out a way of selling more widgets than your team members and, if you did, keeping your methods a secret? Or would you work together with your fellow sales force team members, in the knowledge that the team's success may not keep you in a job?

Perceptions of organizational fairness as a whole

Fairness is not a clear-cut concept for organizations. People will look at issues of fairness on multiple levels – organizational, team and individual. What seems like a fair decision at one level may appear patently unfair at another.

Take an example which is very relevant given the difficult economic circumstances most organizations are operating under at the moment. Senior managers may have to make a section of the workforce redundant, which from their position appears to be a fair decision, taken to benefit a majority at the expense of minority. Certainly, for the people made redundant this may seem unfair. However, to the people who from senior management's perspective should be thankful, if they are then all told that they cannot have a pay rise, but need to work harder to make up for the work of those people laid off – that may not seem very fair to those employees either. And, unless other drivers of discretionary effort are relatively strong, it is unlikely to engender much voluntary additional effort.

A good example of how easy it is to slip up over these kinds of issue is the messaging of the coalition government in the UK when it came into power in 2010. And note that what follows is in no way pro or anti the coalition government, merely an observation on its messaging strategy.

The government was faced with some difficult decisions in the light of a growing budget deficit, high levels of national debt, and the impact on the UK economy of the economic difficulties of other nations, notably the Eurozone. The difficult decision was taken to implement what were widely tagged as 'austerity' measures. An unpalatable decision politically, possibly – but in the coalition's opinion a necessary policy.

While it was always going be difficult to sell such a policy to the public, the coalition's choice of language did not make their task any easier. A clear statement was made by the British Prime Minister, David Cameron, in his first speech as

Prime Minister to the Conservative Party conference that 'we are all in this together'. A speech that hammered home the togetherness theme – a theme that was subsequently picked up by the media.

What followed, however, were a number of policy statements and actions that appeared to suggest that rather than all being 'in it together' one section of society was being less adversely affected than others. Whether it was taxation, pay and bonuses, child benefit, university fees, working hours, pensions, petrol prices, energy bills, and much more, the perception was that we were not all in it together. Furthermore, the Prime Minister and Chancellor of the Exchequer and much of the cabinet were portrayed as coming from privileged backgrounds, privately-educated and wealthy. There were accusations that the Government was relatively unaffected by the changes made in the name of austerity, and immune to the economic pain felt by large sections of the populous.

There was a widespread feeling of unfairness among some sections of society, some commentators even suggested it may have been a contributing factor to the rioting in London, and elsewhere in the UK, in the summer of 2011. Even if not, the sense of unfairness resulting from the difference between 'we are all in it together' and the reality of people's everyday lives, made it more difficult for the government to roll out other policies it believed necessary for the good of the UK, such as 'the Big Society'. This policy, about people pulling together to provide services in their communities, requires and relies upon considerable discretionary effort from the public. Discretionary effort that is less likely to be forthcoming if there is a widespread feeling that the very segments of society required to participate are being unfairly disadvantaged by government policies.

Procedural justice

Procedural justice is a concept that relates to the structures and procedures within an organization, and employee evaluations of the fairness and quality of decision-making processes and company structure. More broadly, it raises issues of equity and fairness in the workplace. A clear message that came back from the research was the link between procedural justice and the likelihood of an individual providing their discretionary effort.

It is a subject that does not appear to be talked or written about much. Certainly, compared to leadership, communication, or many of the management soft skills, when it comes to issues of equity and fairness the bookshelves are relatively empty. But, while people may be less inclined to put pen to paper about the subject, its effects are frequently encountered within organizations.

Employees are more willing to go the extra mile when they perceive that the organization and the managers that they deal with are fair – both in the way that they are dealt with, and in the way that things are structured. Unfortunately, though, there are many ways that unfairness can manifest itself. A sense of injustice can stem from the slightest matter, something that may appear hugely trivial and petty to an uninvolved observer.

I might be filled with rancour and bitterness because someone else had more biscuits than I did in the coffee break, for example. And, as a result, I may therefore be less inclined to do more. Okay, so that example is obviously slightly tongue in cheek, but such apparently unimportant matters can start wars, let alone damaging rifts in the office. Honduras and El

Salvador fought a four-day war triggered by a football match. The flourishing of a severed ear in Parliament was enough justification to start an 18th century war between Great Britain and Spain – the War of Jenkins' ear.

In an organizational setting, I have heard of a situation in one office, for example, where a group of people alienated themselves from the rest of the office because they kept nipping off for a couple of biscuits. It wasn't a whole office thing but a self-selected group. The rest of the office resented them because they were left to work while the select group gossiped and munched on their HOBNOB biscuits. If they asked you to join the biscuit club and you declined they mocked you. If you did join them the rest of the office resented you. Cigarette breaks are another bone of contention especially when people disappear on cigarette breaks, leaving the disgruntled non-smokers, who have no additional breaks allocated, to cover for them back in the office.

And that is without even discussing issues that most would consider far more important to the good functioning of the organization, and potentially even more divisive. Issues such as salary and reward, roles and responsibilities, promotion prospects, or the amount of work an individual does.

In fact a sense of injustice and unfairness can arise from almost anything it seems. While some things may be more obvious it is not always easy to predict what will give rise to discontent. One thing is for certain, however, if managers and leaders allow the feelings of unfairness, inequity and injustice to persist, they can really fester and poison the atmosphere of a team, a business unit and, if entrenched or widespread, even an organization. And, if it remains untreated, this kind of deep-seated perception of unfairness certainly puts paid to the prospects of getting discretionary effort from people in the organization.

While many managers acknowledge the need to tackle this issue, a common response is often similar to that of one executive we spoke with: 'I hear a lot of that. About things not being fair. I hear it from employees. But then I hear it from my children. Sometimes I think it is something that people need to get over, because life just isn't fair.' But this attitude overlooks the possible effects of perceived fairness on performance, even at a low level.

Not that I want to confuse fairness with equality. Not everyone is equal within organizations. There may be equality of opportunity – but completely non-hierarchical organizations are virtually non-existent. And, when asked about the issue of unequal effort in teams, or internal job applications which are ostensibly open, but where the candidate has already been selected, the same executive was quick to stress that such unfairness had to be dealt with.

People that are not pulling their weight

Perhaps one of the most common causes of people feeling a sense of injustice relates to the relative performance of people in the same team. Most people have worked in a team where not everyone makes an equal contribution to the team's performance. Maybe they are reluctant to help their colleagues. Maybe they are lazy. Maybe they don't like to answer calls. Most of us have met people who somehow always manage to be where the work isn't.

We can witness it first hand in almost any department store in the world. There are those who are quick to engage with the customer and offer assistance, and there are others who actively avoid eye contact and try to look busy with an important task when really they just can't be bothered. When you are eventually able to force some form of dialogue, perhaps you have interrupted them talking about their weekend, they are curt and unhelpful. How dare we interrupt them!

Or it may be that, through no fault of their own, they have had a lot more sickness leave. Or because of flexible working arrangements, don't appear to be in the office, and certainly not for those long evenings, and occasional weekends, when you are finishing up an important project to try to meet a deadline.

While this may not bother some people, for others it creates a sense of injustice that grates on them.

'It is a destroyer of discretionary effort. If you have a team, and there's one or two members of the team who are not performing and that's not addressed, over time it will erode confidence in the leadership and the purpose. People will reduce their effort. They will wonder why they should bother, because it isn't being addressed.

'So it is an important thing to get right, being timely and firm with those kinds of interventions. The wrong behaviours cannot be tolerated, behaviour outside of what the agreed cultural norms are, because that is a form of poor performance. Nor can poor quality of work, or less effort than is appropriate. If those things are not addressed, then it really is a destroyer. So it's really important. You've got to get it right, and to treat those people firmly and fairly, and intervene in a timely way.'

Organizations must be seen to be doing something about the matter. If, however, someone fails to pull their weight, nothing is done about it, and they continue to be rewarded on the same basis as the rest of the team who are, effectively, carrying that individual, there is very likely to be a problem. All the hard work you have put in to create a team with a sense of purpose, pulling in the same direction, will start to unravel. People will get angry. It affects performance generally, and definitely impacts on discretionary effort. If you asked them whether they were likely to do a little bit more than they needed to, they might easily reply: 'why should I bother?'

So whether it is someone's letting the side down because they are not mucking in and helping out, whether they are delivering poor customer service, or they are racking up a disproportionate amount of sickness absence, that situation needs to be managed. Not just for the sake of the person in question, but for the sake of the team that they work with, and the organization as a whole.

Favouritism

It doesn't have to be a lack of effort that causes problems, of course. The unequal treatment of employees can happen for many reasons and in many circumstances. Bad behaviour from an individual, poorly dealt with by a manager, can soon lead to wider problems in a team. Employees are usually very aware of the way individual members of the team are treated by managers and quick to notice any differences in approach or attitude.

'You have to make sure that if you're going to inspire a culture where discretionary effort is given freely and naturally, then you really have to make sure that you never appear to display favouritism', one manager told us.

'You have got to be very consistent, it has got to be really visible, it has got to be tangible so people feel that regardless of who is involved in something, what the background is, the view from the sidelines will be fair, and they must be able to trust that. The last thing you want is an environment where there is a bunch of favourites, and a bunch of the rest. That just fights against what you're aiming at.'

So it is important for the manager not to exhibit favouritism. We have all had bosses who have 'stolen' your genius idea and passed it off as their own. It happens all of the time and it's incredibly frustrating. But when a manager appears to be choosing who shines and who is left battling against the current it can turn from frustration to something far more destructive. It is important for the leader to visibly demonstrate even-handedness.

And, just as the leaders can create a sense injustice through their actions in the case of showing favouritism, so they can also foster a sense of unfairness through lack of action.

Another common cause of perceptions of unfairness can occur when people doing similar jobs have very different terms and conditions. This can often arise, for example, after a merger or acquisition, or corporate restructuring.

We spoke to one person who worked for an organization where, at one point, there were two businesses that made up the group, and people in these businesses were treated very differently. More recently, however, they have begun to level the playing field relating to harmonized terms, conditions, and benefits across the two businesses. 'We've continued to harmonize some of the things that weren't harmonized between the two businesses, and treat everybody fairly, showing genuine care and concern. This has had a huge positive effect in terms of respect, [and presumably trust]', they told us.

'It has also encouraged people to think about actions taken by the management in terms of the impact on the organization rather than the individual. So, for example, a decision to change the way that company cars are leased – and company cars are a hugely emotive issue in many workplaces – is greeted with an understanding that it is good for the business, rather than an absolute uproar because people viewed it as something being taken away from them.'

Tackling inequity

One main weapon in the fight against unfairness, is to make sure that there is a robust, well thought out performance management system in place, and that it is implemented properly, especially when the source of that unfairness concerns someone not pulling their weight, or poor behaviour or, indeed, rewards and recognition. First, though, before you can manage the problem you have to detect it. This comes partly through the general lines of communication a manager has with their team and also through the appraisal process.

'Number one, you should be looking for those situations. Checking whether they are real or perceived. So, as a leader, it is important that you are aware if that is happening. Everything is not always going to be even and fair. But you want to look for the egregious cases of disparity or resentment', said one manager in a multinational business services firm. 'Assuming that it is real, you need to do something about it. Then you need to subtly address it by adjusting expectations or assigning and aligning responsibilities in a different way. So I think you can orchestrate that.'

Line managers play a crucial and sometimes very difficult role here. Dealing with an issue where someone is not doing their bit, or a person's poor performance is affecting the team's performance, is not an easy management task. It requires leaders to separate any desire to be liked, from the need to tackle unfairness and have some tough conversations.

As one manager explained to us: 'It is not about being nice to everybody all the time. It is absolutely about being equitable. So, if somebody steps out of line, then you jump on that but explain the reasons why, for the first couple of times at least. Allow people to make mistakes but, hopefully, not more than once.

'If somebody is having a laugh (taking liberties) then you're going to stamp on that very hard. Otherwise other people, their colleagues, are going to say, well he or she gets away with it so why shouldn't I?'

Or as another manager put it: 'To get the best out of people, and to maximize discretionary effort, you don't have to be everybody's friend. It isn't about being Mr or Mrs Popular, and everybody loving you. That's not what it's about. At all.

'Sometimes I think managers mistake that. They think that they've got to be everybody's friend, to be popular, to be all things to all people. That's a path to failure, in my opinion, because what you end up doing is overlooking poor performance, and not dealing with it in a timely way. Either it becomes huge, and a big issue, and everybody's annoyed, or nothing ever happens.'

The appraisal process will also flag up issues that may lead to problems around fairness. So, for example, take the appraisal process described by one executive in large media organization: 'We have our version of an appraisal where people would get feedback from their line managers or whatever. For developmental purposes in some of the management roles, we also do a 360 feedback, and for the management population, we may do a questionnaire on things like their leadership, where their direct reports will comment on their leadership capability, so they can get feedback.'

This, as the executive notes, is fairly standard, and hopefully during this process any issues around an individual falling short of their peer's expectations would come to light.

Managing expectations

To begin with, leaders need to get to the bottom of why someone is underperforming compared to their peers, as there may be very good reasons for the individual's behaviour, which can be relatively easily addressed.

A common problem is for there to be misunderstandings related to the goals, responsibilities and expectations involved, both generally as a team and more specifically as an individual. Often teams fail because the journey towards the best possible outcome has not been communicated and agreed.

That does not mean that each individual needs to know the goals of all their team members in detail. However, people do need to understand broadly what other people in the team are responsible and accountable for, and what they are working towards. So that everyone has a really good sense of what the team is trying to accomplish.

Then, once someone has a good, broad understanding of what the different members of the team are doing and are responsible for, they need to be clear exactly what is expected of them by their manager.

One executive was very clear about how this needs to work, and what leaders need to do, in order to minimize underperformance by individuals stemming from misunderstanding of role and responsibilities.

'Once you have clear goals, and everyone understands what the team members are supposed to be doing, then it is important that the manager is clear about the expectations with the employee. Because a lot of times it can be that the employee may not be pulling their weight because they don't understand what they're supposed to be doing. So that's why we make sure that we have clearly written goals and responsibilities.'

Performance plan

Alongside the need to delineate roles and responsibilities very clearly in the first instance – and then continue to make sure that they are updated as required – there also needs to be a very robust and rigorous performance management programme or plan. So, if an individual is not pulling their weight, and it is not due to a misunderstanding about goals and objectives, and what is expected of an individual, the manager can move onto the next stage of tackling the issue.

As the same executive explained: 'We have what is called a performance plan. A plan that we put in place to try to help the employee through the challenges that they may be having. It's not necessarily a negative thing. It could just be that a person needs more training, or that they need a better understanding of how to build stakeholder engagement, for example. But it is incumbent upon the manager that, if they explain the goals, if they have been very clear, if they have worked on a performance plan, and then you get to the point that something doesn't happen as a result, then you are going to have to make a tough decision about whether the employee's really suited for the role or not.'

In other words, if someone is not pulling their weight, and a manager has exhausted all the possibilities for this, explored remedies including moving them to another team or role (where possible), and there is still no change, then that individual will need to be managed out.

As we said earlier in this chapter, failure to do this will have a negative impact on the others within the team as they begin to resent the underperformance of the individual in question.

Drivers in Action: Procedural Justice

Quick Intervention

'When you are managing poor performance the speed of the intervention is essential.

'So I think that it is about getting people's respect, and being prepared to step in early and have the conversations early. If you do this and the patient doesn't respond to treatment correctly, then you need to put some alternative strategies in place quickly, but you do it fairly. By the book. But don't mess about.

'As I've managed people now for over 20 years, over time I've probably got quicker at intervening. So, as an experienced manager, you probably give people more chance, but are probably firmer, but that doesn't mean unfair or unjust.

'When you sit people down early, before the problem gets bigger one of two things happens. Either the performance is resolved more quickly, or the person leaves sooner. Either way you get a better outcome more quickly, and that's for the greater good.'

An executive in a major pharmaceutical company

The internal promotion process

Just as it helps to be transparent about overall objectives at an organizational, operational unit, or team unit, so it helps to be transparent about more specific matters. In Semco, the Brazilian organization transformed by Ricardo Semler, (featured in Chapter 3), the salaries of staff were displayed for other staff to see.

Incidentally, in many Scandinavian countries – Sweden, Finland and Norway, for example – tax returns are public records which can be inspected by anybody. Perhaps coincidentally, Sweden, Norway and Finland are in the top ten countries (out of 178) perceived as the least corrupt, according to Transparency International's 2010 Corruption Perceptions Index. The United Kingdom is 20th and the United States of America 22nd. (Sweden and Finland are also the third and fourth most competitive countries in the world according to the World Economic Forum's Global Competitiveness Index 2011–2012 rankings.)

While most firms will balk at openly publishing the salaries of employees, it is certainly possible to be more open about career development and talent management. And this may help to eliminate potential misunderstandings and confusion about career paths and promotions as well as about roles and responsibilities.

In one well-known leisure industry organization, the manager we spoke with told us about the personal development planning process in their organization and the transparency built into the process.

'Everyone has what's called a personal development plan, which lays out their career. They work with their manager on that, on what are the next steps, what are the things they want to develop, where they want to go. The important thing is that we identify and socialize that so that it is not hidden. So people know what I'm interested in, and where I want to go. If you just take me as an example, not only do I have that plan in place with my manager, but my manager is very good about saying to others where I want to go.'

The same principle of transparency should apply to internal job applications. 'Transparency is absolutely huge. If you're not transparent about what you're doing, it can cause all sorts of problems. If we are going to restructure, and some people are in a closed pool to apply for certain jobs, or people are invited to apply for jobs. Or if you have got a new vacancy and it is not advertised, for whatever reason. This is where I think that you can serve to disengage people unless you're very clear about the reasons why you have taken a certain course of action.'

Reward and recognition

In the same way, equity and fairness must be seen to be at work when organizations are drawing up and implementing reward and recognition policies. One of the executives we spoke with explained how they ensure a degree of fairness in their rewards and recognition.

'If we take reward and recognition, one of the things we have across our contact centres is a recognition which is called Fame. It is used as a thank you for something someone has done, something where they have gone slightly out of their way to do something, and this is entirely equitable.

'For a Fame Award you get a little badge and you can fit it on a lanyard with your security pass on it, so it's visible for all to see. You can have one of these whether you were the most senior manager, or whether you were someone that's only been in the company a week. So it's equitable in that it spans all layers and all types of jobs, and it's something that is really just a thank you, so actually in this context it is most often used for discretionary effort.'

In addition, says the executive, in many organizations equity and fairness are written into the rules when there are incentives to meet a particular target. So, in this case, an organization should be asking questions like – can everyone participate, and is the rewards and incentives system administered fairly?

Drivers in Action: Procedural Justice

Clear and Candid

One of the main ways that organizations can address inequity and unfairness at a general level is through transparency and openness.

One executive related their experience of having to make some very difficult staffing decisions in their organization. Because of financial constraints it was necessary to make half the team redundant, and lose not far short of 100 people. But, as the executive explained, the redundancy process went as well as could be expected given such a difficult and emotive task. From all the redundancies only one case proved problematic.

The reason for this comparative lack of problem was, they said, because everything was explained, everything was open. Any restructured jobs were properly advertised. Management met with people individually, and as groups, and gave adequate time to discuss the situation with people. And although there were, unsurprisingly, people who were upset and certainly didn't want to leave the organization, the process went as smoothly as could be expected given the circumstances.

As the executive added: 'I don't think that you can have procedural justice unless your HR team, the handling of salaries, appraisals, employment, the deployment of people, and so on, are very open, very transparent, and share what the current thinking is all the time.'

Playing fair

Many organizations include concepts like equity, justice, fairness and so on, in their values statements. For those organizations it is time to make sure they really do live up to those values. And for those organizations that have not given much thought to this issue, it is time to focus on fairness.

As one executive that we spoke to, who is responsible for workplace engagement, explained to us:

'That sense of justice is an important value to your whole organization. It might be, for example, that someone wants to join the company and wants to stay because they know it is an important value for that organization, so then they are going to be more willing to go the extra mile. Or if you sense that something isn't fair, in a way it inhibits what you are prepared to do; so there's a reluctance.'

After all – why should employees play fair if the business isn't fair to them?

Fair's Fair – Action Points

At the root of this driver are the systems and processes your organization has set up. Performance assessment, promotion paths, pay, rewards, recognition, annual leave allocation and all the other systems to assess, remunerate and reward employees need to be transparent and fair to the staff. If individuals believe that the business creates procedures that treat them unfairly compared to other team members or employees, they are unlikely to fight to go the extra mile.

The power to change deeply embedded companywide processes and systems may lie with the most senior managers, but beyond this there are one or two things an individual manager can do to foster a culture with justice at its core.

1. Listening meetings – a specific time to listen not to brief

Stuff at work happens.

Tops aren't getting the info they need; Middles and Bottoms aren't getting the direction they need; Customers aren't getting the attention they need.

Work on projects get started, gets taken away, disappears into a black hole, the organization appears disjointed. Middles can't get their act together, there are imbalances, some projects draw lots of attention others get little or none.

Tops are invisible to bottoms who wonder what, if anything, tops do; reorganizations happen and many wonder why. Bottoms wonder what the value of Middles is. Tops are deluged by demands from every direction, Middles get bonuses they feel they don't deserve and don't get bonuses they feel they do deserve.

It's another day of 'white water', emotions run the full gamut – from excitement and challenge to anger, despair, hopelessness and apathy. And then it's time to start listening to each other.

Get together regularly – the whole team and other stakeholders/departments – and encourage everyone to describe their world for everyone else. Use the following structure:

- What are the issues you are dealing with?
- What are you feeling?
- How are you seeing other parts of the business? Are they helping or hindering you?
- What do you most need?

2. Understanding the whole

As each part of the business or system begins to elucidate its world for the others, together they illuminate the whole. It's as if someone has turned on the lights for the whole system.

There are four basic guidelines to ensure that each department begins to see and understand the other:

1. Tell the truth (paint a picture for us, you are the experts in your part of the system, there is no other way for us to know what your world is like).
2. Listen carefully (don't argue or debate, just let it in).
3. Everyone turns up (all relevant parties are important, whether you are satisfied or dissatisfied, ready for new challenges or ready to quit, your experience is relevant for the process, come and be prepared to share your experiences).
4. No business (this is not a staff meeting; it is not a time to solve problems although this often comes out of the listening process. The purpose is to illuminate the system for all).

3. Talk straight, be fair, and treat everyone equally

As a manager, your staff will watch you; they will want to see that how you are with them, matches how you are with everyone else. It will be important to them that you have not got any favourites and that you value everyone equally. Look at the relationships you have with all your staff and ask yourself:

- Do I spend as much time with each member of my team?
- Do I balance the non-work and work conversations in the right proportions and equally amongst all staff?
- Are my messages clear and consistent from team member to team member?
- Which relationship could I work on straight away?

You may not have much influence on the machine that is the business you work for but you do have the ability to be fair with your team.

4. Attitudes and perceptions

Remember, fairness is not just about setting up processes that are fair. It is also essential that the employees see the managers, and the organization as a whole, acting in a fair way. Perceptions are everything. The key to making this happen is transparency and openness. It may not be a natural part of the organization's culture, but at every point, with very few exceptions, managers should adopt a policy of transparency and openness as a default position.

7.   TEAM TALK

'I am a member of a team, and I rely on the team, I defer to it and sacrifice for it, because the team, not the individual, is the ultimate champion.'

Mia Hamm

Each year, UK retail giant Sainsbury's holds an event for around 5000 of its staff. I have been fortunate enough to work at the event on a number of occasions and each time I have been impressed by how the sense of team filters through the various areas of the business. In some way or another every individual attending considers themselves part of a team. Be that their small team within a store, the store as a whole, their colleague forum or, most commonly, the organization generally.

Throughout the year the senior leadership team works hard to maximize engagement levels amongst its 150,000 employees. Initiatives designed to enhance teamwork are embraced by the individual stores and then celebrated at their annual event. To call it an event is, in fact, somewhat misleading. In many ways this gathering together of colleagues from around the UK is an interactive show with delegates moving from one experience to another.

In 2011, for example, there was an area the size of three football pitches displaying cheeses, cakes, biscuits, drinks, games, decorations and all of the other products expected for Christmas. There was a catwalk where Gok Wan, the UK TV presenter of *How to Look Good Naked*, showcased his new fashion line commissioned by the business. The 50 models? All volunteer Sainsbury's employees.

Each of the individual stores is proud of its own identity and each of the 1000 stores is represented; yet they all pull for the business together. Staff from head office are encouraged to adopt a store that they would like to support, and they then get involved with that store far more than their day-to-day role would typically legislate for. I have walked around this event, set in the enormous National Exhibition Centre in Birmingham and seen CEO, Justin King, embraced as one of the team by everyone there from the fishmongers to the deliverymen. Seldom, in my travels, do I witness this level of mutual respect between colleagues and sense that they are 'all in it together'.

My role during the day was twofold. Firstly I hosted the Paralympic Village where three sports were demonstrated in a purpose-built, 1500-seat sports arena. The business then also takes the opportunity to celebrate success via their Stars Awards which, after a quick change backstage, I hosted. These awards cover many of the traditional areas of business focus but also champion undertakings that are less directly linked to financial targets.

Of course there are strong commercial reasons for holding an event such as this – increasing profitability, reducing staff turnover, or deriving-maximum benefit from the supermarket retailer's sponsorship of the 2012 Paralympics, but these genuinely feel secondary to the goal of creating unity amongst the businesses colleagues.

Teams and discretionary effort

Teams are an essential part of organizational life. They exist in many different forms and cover many different types of organizational activity. There is the executive board, the senior management team and, in a large organization, there may be teams of functional heads. There are functional teams, such as sales and marketing, finance, or logistics. Plus there are project teams within functions, as well as cross-functional teams. Teams don't have to be face-to-face, of course. In an increasing globalized economy teams are often dispersed across cities, countries, and continents.

Teams also play an important role in encouraging or discouraging discretionary effort. Another important driver of discretionary effort identified by the research is team identification. In this context, identification refers to the extent to which an individual feels that they belong to a team. That identification stems from the behaviour and influence of others around the individual. So, for example the behaviour of other team members may make an employee proud to be in the same team. Perhaps they are inspired by the excellent customer service offered by colleagues or they like the way everyone pulls together when under pressure. Of course poor behaviour can have the opposite effect. If corners are cut and duties shirked people are much less likely to want to be associated with a team.

Whatever it is that creates a stronger sense of belonging, it appears that the more closely someone identifies with their team, then the more likely they are to go the extra mile. And so that creates a challenge, both for team members and for team leaders, with regards to the kinds of things that can be done to create a sense of team identification. How can the organization help to make people feel they are really part of team?

Drivers in Action: Team Identification

Proud to be on Your Team

'The idea that you could be proud of your CEO, proud of your leader, is not something that gets talked about very much. And I think probably if you were genuinely proud of your boss, or genuinely proud to say I'm proud to be part of this team, or I'm proud to work for this business, the amount of discretionary effort that would bring I'm sure would be huge.'

A manager in a large multimedia organization

Team means different things to different people

There is an example I often use to illustrate people's different perspectives on teams. It may be reasonably well known, but it is a powerful story nevertheless.

During the space race, in the 1960s, President John F. Kennedy took a tour of NASA. Stopping occasionally to talk to the employees the President asked one man: 'What's your job at the facility?' The man replied: 'My job is to help put a man on the moon'. The man was a janitor. However, he had a point. He clearly understood that every single person at NASA had a role to play.

Neil Armstrong later said, as he stepped onto the moon, 'That's one small step for a man, one giant leap for mankind', it was a leap that would never have taken place unless the whole of the team at NASA believed that their contribution mattered. Each person had to identify with the team and their task regardless of their role, and the janitor was as much of the team as the top scientists or the astronauts.

I have been fortunate to experience my own JFK/Janitor moment. Following a successful Sydney Paralympics, the gold medal winning team began to prepare for the next Games. Once you have tasted glory you crave it again. Most gold medal winners will try to defend their medal if they can. So we began to search for ways to swim faster. We knew our competitors would improve, so we needed to improve too.

We re-evaluated what the 'swim team' really meant and conducted a stakeholder analysis. Who impacted on our ability to achieve? Who was in the team? Did they all identify with our desire to retain our Paralympic title? There were a surprisingly large number of people involved beyond the people I saw everyday: doctors, nurses, physiologists, sports psychologists, biomechanists, physiotherapists, team managers, coaches etc. We then began a process of engaging with this broader group, helping them to feel part of the team and to realize how important they were to the process of winning once again.

Four years later in Athens, my last Paralympic Games, the freestyle relay team swam faster than it had ever done before. It was a terrific team performance. But for me, the highlight of that success was not the performance at Athens; it came when I returned. I was at the Manchester Aquatics centre when the duty manager at the pool came up to my coach, Lars Humer, and told him how much he had enjoyed watching the Athens Paralympics on television and how proud he was to see the team doing so well. Then he said 'I *am* part of that team, aren't I?' And he was.

Alignment

One thing very apparent from our research is that the concept of the team is a very broad one. People often belong to more than one team. They will usually be a member of a sub-functional team and the organization as a whole. They may belong to a particular business unit, or region. Or they may be part of a business function team and a product team.

An employee's tasks and objectives as part of a team may vary between teams. Where there is an element of conflict or competition between the teams that an individual belongs to, this can create problems. For example, a product development team may need more time to finish adding extra features to a new product. However, the senior management may consider speed to market more important for the company. If managers are aware of potential conflicts and can align the interests of teams, this can lead to very positive results. With the right alignment of purpose, an employee might feel a strong connection to both their project team, functional team and to the wider organization.

Certainly the executives we spoke to made it clear that it is important to think beyond a person's immediate team when thinking about team identification. One manager, for example, told us how people felt loyalty towards a particular function in the organization.

'Why do people want to work in finance, for example? They don't say that it is because of the leadership, or the recognition, or their personal development. It is because they feel as though they are part of a community', the manager told us.

'So the finance people get together. They do a show at the Christmas Year End event. The finance team are always the team that seem to go out to dinner together. There's definitely a culture that's being built there. There is a culture that's being built in finance that is based around working more cohesively and more effectively together.

'That is reflected in their professional development. The people in finance are really moved across a range of elements that make up the finance function. So everybody gets an opportunity to learn about treasury, for example. And by moving the finance people around you continue to emphasize the community element – over the silo mindset. People don't feel siloed, but part of the larger community.'

Equally, people can identify with the organization as a whole. And organizations should take steps to encourage this. This might be through the vision and values, for example. When one company involved in the mail and parcels business decided to articulate its vision and values it elected to do so in a way that its employees could easily identify with.

Rather than use the terms 'vision' and 'values' the firm chose to talk about destination and journey. 'What we wanted was something that was simple and very tangible for our business. So we created a very simple, one page destination: this is who we are; this is what we do; this is where we do it; this is why we do it; and this is how we do it. Just five bullet points. Then the journey is about delivering great service for our customers every time, and here we interpret customers as being both internal and external to the business – so respect each other, and work and win.'

But then, said the executive, they also chose to highlight the phrase 'great, together, now.' 'We are great together now, and that is what matters. Living that and bringing it to life has really helped. People not only respect each other here more, as a result, but they also respect the brand more', she continued.

As this executive and many others realized while some people think of team in a very narrow way, if you look at team broadly, everyone is in an organization, everyone is on the same team, and in that sense everyone is on a journey together.

Drivers in Action: Team Identification

Celebrating Together

A good example of how companies can build team identity at an organizational level is the way that one company celebrated its first birthday.

For a start there were cupcakes for all the several thousand employees. It was a small gesture but a fun one, and more importantly an inclusive one.

The firm also created a series of achievement rooms, gathering together all the various accomplishments from the first year, to remind its employees of their achievements so far.

In addition to this the firm also set aside a section of its intranet where people posted up all the things that they had done for the first time that year. At the same time the company also posted up all the things that it had achieved as a company for the first time that year. The firm also compiled a video, which highlighted its achievements.

And then there was a birthday card competition in which employees and their families were encouraged to get involved and come up with a design for the firm's birthday card. It was organized in four age groups so that children could be involved. Every employee received one of the four designs, each containing a flavour of the firm's achievements for the year and a message from the CEO.

Finally, the company ran various road shows for the field staff at which the cupcakes were handed out, as were various goodies branded with the firm's values. The whole event was run over a week, giving everyone a chance to get involved, and was combined with recognition awards.

On your team

On the 11 December 2005 there was one word on the lips of every British firefighter: 'Buncefield'. At 6:01am the Buncefield oil storage facility, located near the M1 in Hertfordshire, exploded. The terminal was the fifth largest oil-products storage depot in the United Kingdom, with a capacity of about 272,765,400 litres of fuel.

The first and largest explosion measured 2.4 on the Richter scale, and led to further explosions, eventually overwhelming 20 large storage tanks. The emergency services announced a major emergency and a firefighting effort began.

At peak times this effort consisted of 25 fire engines, 20 support vehicles and 180 firefighters. Around 150 firefighters were called immediately to the incident, and began tackling the blaze. Initial assessment concluded that the incident would be the largest fire of its type in the world ever to be fought by a fire brigade, and foam supplies from sites all over the UK were called upon.

Six high-volume pumps were used to extract 25,000 litres of water per minute from a reservoir 1.5 miles from the fire, with six more high-volume pumps deployed at various locations to serve as boosters. Around 32,000 litres per minute of firefighting foam were directed against the fire.

Teamwork is important within virtually every organization, but when the lives of both the people you serve and your team are at stake then it is essential. This is certainly the case for the fire service.

Teamwork improves levels of safety, accountability and efficiency. Firefighters know their respective responsibilities in any given situation and it is of utmost importance in the fire service culture that all individuals contribute to the effort. That lives depend on their ability to perform is ingrained in all firefighters.

Most of their procedures, pieces of equipment and techniques require multiple firefighters. Firefighters never enter a burning structure alone. And, once inside, they depend on their teammates outside to supply enough water – not only to put out the fire but to protect them.

Teamwork at this level of intensity requires trust among its members, and familiarity with one another is the first step in gaining that trust. Providing teams with the ability to interact with each other develops familiarity and the way firefighters operate provides the perfect setting for this opportunity. Firefighters train, eat, and work together, allowing interaction on various levels, both formal and informal.

Training sessions provide an arena in which to discover talents within the group, as older, more experienced members share their knowledge with less experienced members of the team. Everyone can see what is expected and quickly see what other firefighters are capable of.

Non-training periods, such as mealtimes, allow team members to learn about each other's backgrounds, beliefs, and experiences in a casual setting. This way of living and working bonds fire teams together and clearly influences their ability to cope with situations such as the one in Buncefield.

Firefighting teams are exceptional. They need to be able to cope with the most adverse situations. Yet, as we will see in the next few sections, the same team identification principles that are so important in building a firefighting team are just as relevant for teams in other organizations, whether it is a niche financial services firm in a highly competitive market, a public sector healthcare firm, a giant multinational, a non-governmental organization or a social enterprise.

Knowledge share

Perhaps one of the most obvious ways of building a sense of team identity is through gathering together and sharing information. The sharing can involve anything from issues about work, planning team activities, complimenting individuals on their accomplishments, or discussing what people did at the weekend. Stories are a powerful way of building a sense of common interest, and it is important that enough time is spent on sharing these for everybody to feel part of the team.

Sharing information can be a formal team-specific exercise. So, in one organization for example, individual team members discuss their individual, personal values, and then compare notes with their colleagues to see how those values are similar or very different. They look at what is most important to them, and what matters the least. Together they explore the team values as a whole, and what that means for the way the team works and is perceived. Thus the team is aware of how the values of team members and the team collectively align, building greater team identification.

Often it is the HR department that gets involved in embedding articulated values into the way the organization works, and gets involved in other aspects of team development. So, HR may be the first port of call for team leaders wanting to work on team identification.

The key thing is to make time for the team to discuss issues collectively. Consulting firm Fairplace Cedar worked with academics at Cass Business School, to develop a team building process. The intervention uses a research based questionnaire to assess team performance over a range of criteria. The findings from the survey are then used as a basis for a facilitated meeting to discuss how the team can improve. One of the most remarkable aspects revealed by this process, however, is the number of teams that do not have collective discussion about team dynamics, overall goals and objectives, and how best to achieve them. So many teams are focused on immediate tasks and short-term goals to the exclusion of all else.

So getting the team together for something more than a quick performance check-up is essential. Team meetings do not need to be held on the organization's premises either; often the best solution from a team bonding perspective is to take people offsite, whether it is just for a day or two, or a longer period.

Take one company executive we spoke to, who is both a member of a senior team, and leads their own team of over 100 people, the majority dispersed across the US. Both teams will communicate frequently through a variety of media, but also ensure that they schedule face-to-face time to help with team bonding.

The executive meets with the senior team on a quarterly basis. These three-monthly meetings are usually two to three days in length, and also usually away from the building, so that people are not distracted by their day-to-day work. (Some organizations will restrict access to mobile communications during such meetings as well.) In the case of this particular company and senior team there is always a team building component included as well.

'HR often helps us to facilitate the team building component, in terms of how we work better together. A lot of times we will do things like personality profiling, for example, or we will work with executive coaches. We specifically try to drill down on the things that this team needs. It is easy to do team building and it is just generic – you know, let's all get together and do a fun thing – but we really try to drill down and ask, "okay, what is this team's strengths and what are their weaknesses and how do we develop this particular team?"

Then, in addition to the quarterly senior team meetings, the executive tries to bring his own team of direct reports together, as well as the entire team he is responsible for, on a regular, even if infrequent basis. It is a challenge, especially given a situation where there is a widely distributed team – in this case 80% of the executive's team is based throughout the United States, not where the executive is based.

'We're a global company and my directors could also be field based. So I have ten direct reports and four of them are field based. What we hear a lot is that the face-to-face time is still important. So that is a big thing for us.

'I do one annual team meeting where I bring over 100 people together for a week. And, if we are investing in bringing everyone together, we want to maximize that time. So, in that meeting we try to do several things.

'One thing is to provide updates on key initiatives, so that the whole team feels really engaged about where the entire group is going and they understand what all their colleagues are doing. We also make sure that we bring in outside speakers from other corporate departments, so that the group gets a broader sense of what's going on within the company. Then we also try to bring an outside speaker, motivational speakers, for example. So one speaker that we had, that was particularly good, spoke about empowerment. So that was another area that we focused on – team building type activities so that the groups feel engaged.'

As someone who spends the vast majority of their time working at events such as this you'll not be surprised that I completely agree with this. In my experience the events that deliver a balance of celebrating success, company updates, internal best practice and external insight have the best impact on the delegates. Combined with provocative follow up this level of information sharing can have a positive impact back in the work place that lasts for months.

Formal team building events

Formal team building activities, often organized in conjunction with external suppliers, can also be a very valuable way of boosting team identity. One person we spoke to could still remember, very vividly, a team building activity that they had participated in in the Lake District in the UK. The task was for the group to build a raft from various items and then sail it out onto a lake. The person we interviewed wasn't that keen on going out onto the lake and initially was reluctant to take part.

However, a desire to contribute to the team's efforts changed that. 'At the end of the session, I was on the raft, and in the water. You do get caught up in what the team's doing and wanting to do things for the greater good of the team. Having one person standing on the shore going, "oh, no, I don't really want to do that," doesn't quite work, does it? If you have a team that are really bonding well together, you will push yourself to do things that you never thought you would do, and I think you can take that into the workplace.'

Many organizations already use these types of formal team building mechanism, but if your organization does not, good firms that provide these services are not difficult to find. And many of these firms have been providing team building type services for a surprisingly long time.

Take the Brathay Hall Trust, as just one small example. This organization has been running team building programmes at the Brathay estate in the Lake District in the UK since the 1940s. Located on the shores of Windermere, Brathay works with all levels of employee and with a variety of organizations in both the private and public sector. And, understandably, many of its team building activities involve the lake.

'We have eight whaler boats, for example, which we use on the lake', says Jez Anderson, head of adult development. 'In essence you are doing an orienteering course in these big rowing boats. That can take place on a beautiful sunny day, or when it is raining or blowing a gale, or even at night in the pitch black. It is all about individuals taking ownership, taking control, being accountable for their actions as part of a team. Then coming back and using that experience to think about what they have learnt, either about being in a team, or being the leader in a team, issues around followership, or conflict or communication, whatever we are trying to explore.'

So team building can be both a lot of fun as well as a highly productive way of feeding stronger team identity and discretionary effort

Team responsibilities

Having spent a large part of my life as a swimmer in a tightly knit swimming team, perhaps the team identification aspect of discretionary effort is an area that I understand the most at a personal level. And that includes understanding the importance of team responsibilities.

One of my favourite stories is about the 1996 Atlanta Paralympics. I was part of a swimming team which was beaten into second place by 12 one-hundredths of a second. I was devastated. However, as with any other competition, I went through a thorough process of review and evaluation, to see what could be learnt and improved upon.

Eventually I watched the race back including the medal ceremony; previously I'd always stopped the tape before that point as I hadn't thought it relevant to the review process. On this occasion though, for no particular reason, I let the tape run on. At that moment I discovered the root of the problem. There we were, the four members of the relay team on the medal podium with our silver medals round our necks – two of us with beaming smiles on our faces; two of us looking devastated.

It was then I realized what was wrong. We didn't share the same dream. We were four individuals who hadn't agreed on the best possible outcome. We hadn't competed as a team. We may have looked like a team, but we weren't an efficient team. When the individuals in a team have different objectives, they are unlikely to reach their full potential and in our team, two wanted gold, and nothing less and two were happy with any medal, regardless of the colour.

Understanding your role in a team, how you contribute to the team's wider goals and objectives, and what these goals and objectives are, is all an important part of team identification.

'Everyone needs to understand the accountability across the team. So people know what they are responsible for, and that what they are responsible for influences or impacts on others, and how it contributes to the overall success', one executive told us.

'When problems arise it is about trying to work them out as a team, as opposed to looking for someone to blame. It is about turning a problem or a challenge into an opportunity that brings the team together. It might only be a problem that's affecting one person. But there is no reason we can't tackle it as a group.

'There you are as a team. Tom's working on the technical infrastructure. Karen's working on the content from a learning perspective. Somebody else is working on something completely different. But if Karen has a problem then we will all come together and figure out what we can do to help.'

In order to identify with their team, the team members need to understand their position in the team and their relationship with the other team members. They also need to feel that they are able to tackle problems collectively.

Shared tasks

Another way to encourage team bonding is to introduce processes that bring people together for a similar cause. Larry Bossidy, the former AlliedSignal CEO, longtime GE executive, and author of *Execution: The Discipline of Getting Things Done*, did this when he introduced the Six Sigma quality approach at AlliedSignal.

'I happen to be a proponent of Six Sigma, but it isn't this specific initiative that-matters', Bossidtm once said.

'It is the fact that you cause people all over the business to work together to get the objectives achieved. It isn't just a financial person, or a marketing person, or a manufacturing person, in Six Sigma you need people from all over the business. And once you can get an attitude and culture of people from all segments of the business working together, something that coherently binds people, then that becomes a strength of the organization.'

It was a similar story with some of the other executives I spoke to. 'One of the biggest successes was where we introduced Lean Management into our operation', said one manager. 'Actually having the teams working together to change processes, and taking ownership of those processes, had a huge effect on the effort that then goes into those areas in the future.'

Organizations can also help to build team identification through getting people together for corporate social responsibility activities. Many organizations allow their employees a certain amount of time to do community and charitable work. While this will often be on an individual basis, it is a good idea to encourage work teams to do this together.

'We have seen some great changes in the way our teams have operated, have participated and collaborated around the Teenage Cancer Trust Events', noted one executive who was explaining how some work within the organization for charitable purposes has helped to create a sense of team identity. Helping team members to understand better the roles of their peers has been particularly helpful. For example, once a fundraiser understands the weight the PR team can bring to an event, but also the work required, they tend to call upon them for assistance for the right events at the right time. While another remarked how the company always tried to run community service events to emphasize the importance of not just looking inward, but also outwards toward the community. In doing this they are clearly doing valuable work for the community but also, be it a deliberate ploy or not, providing additional purposes for why a team should work together and therefore identify with each other.

Enter the matrix

As well as focusing on ways to enable people to identify with their team, organizations can also try to eliminate any barriers to team bonding. The rise of a blame culture can quickly erode any sense of team identification, for example. Or poor leadership, where a manager hijacks the ideas of their team, passes them off as their own, and claims any credit.

Perhaps the most obvious obstacles to building a team identity are structural and geographic. Matrix organizational structures, where employees are grouped by both function and product, have become popular, partly as a way of coping with more complicated operations, in large multinationals, for example, and partly inspired by their implementation in companies such as Swiss engineering giant Asea Brown Boveri (ABB).

But while matrix structures may solve some operational issues, they also create challenges around building team identity. In a matrix organization, one of the main difficulties with creating a sense of team identity is that people have multiple reporting lines and are, effectively, in multiple teams. In these cases it can be much harder to create a sense of place or belonging in the organization.

In a large FMCG group you might have individuals who are in several vertical product categories, as well as being a member of a cross category function such as HR or sales and marketing. A person in this example will effectively have three bosses and be a member of three teams. Unlike being a member of the financial community these people can feel divided loyalties and responsibilities. Perhaps more than ever, 'Whose team are you on?' is a legitimate question.

As one executive who worked in a matrix structure told us: 'That's definitely a challenge I think in this particular model, some of the support functions, like HR for example, might feel that they don't belong anywhere. Or indeed, that they belong everywhere.

'So I would have team workshops with the leadership team for one product category. We would spend several days offsite discussing strategy and so on, which was, to a degree, team building. But then the next week I'd be off with another category and a completely different leader and team. And the two leaders would have very different styles, and very different ways of operating.'

In a sense the notion of identifying with your organization and its mission and values, its objectives and goals, becomes particularly important in these types of situation. In fact after explaining the difficulties associated with team identification within a matrix or multiple reporting lines situation, the same executive added: 'At a higher level, it is being passionate about working for your company.'

So, if you identify strongly with the people in the organization, the values of the organization, the culture of the organization, that in itself is a powerful driver of discretionary effort. Along with team identification at lower levels as you drill down through the organization in smaller and smaller units of personnel.

At a distance

Globalization and advances in communications technology have led to an increase in remote working. Work patterns have changed considerably over the last decade. Employees are able to work on the move, from home, or from remote locations around the world.

However, the ability to work remotely means that team members may easily be located in different places and rarely see or even speak to each other. The further we go in terms of remote working and virtual teams, the less opportunity or intention there is to collect people together and assemble them in one place. Even though the most productive way of working is often when people are physically located together. And this appears to be particularly relevant at a time when so many people are choosing to work from home and organizations actively encouraged to reduce costs

So changes in the way organizations and individuals arrange work also create a team identification challenge. This was a challenge many of the people I spoke to as part of the research recognized, and the solution was often to try to get people together in face-to-face situations, even if only irregularly. Or at least to try to replicate the face-to-face experience in the various communications that take place between team members.

'I remember when I was assigned a project bringing together a cross departmental team to solve a particular problem', said one manager. 'What I would have loved to do was to bring those few people from the three different departments together. Put them in a room for two days, and the problem would be solved.

'There's nothing like bringing people together face to face. Even if it is only once a year. Yes, it is a travel expense, but the return on investment on that is huge. Ultimately we will have to work around that, and get the project done with the six people, in six different cities and in three different departments. But it would get done a lot faster if we were together.

'So when you are working in remote teams you will tend to have a little more time for the non-critical business issues, the personal side. When you have a 90-minute conference call you might spend the first few minutes trying to relate personally.'

Drivers in Action: Team Identification

Call Centre Culture

Call centre culture is funded on teams. So it is no surprise to find that team identification plays an important role. 'We recruit them as teams, and we lead them within teams to create the community', says one executive with responsibility for the organization's call centres.

They do a number of things to foster strong team identification amongst the members of the team. 'There are the very basics of the mixture, that the mix of people within the team actually fit really well with the leader. So, some teams have got some very vociferous, open-minded people in them. We make sure that we've got the right sort of person in there to actually engage with that and make the most of it.

'We allow them to live, work and play as teams, so we put them on breaks together. We encourage them through incentives, to actually go out and have fun together, to work and live together and create that sort of philosophy. We try not to change the teams too much. Although quite often the mix of teams can become a little stale, so we introduce new members, just to keep things fresh. And that pays back into the business.'

A senior manager in an IT company

The difference teams make

Most people will appreciate what a difference working in a good team, as opposed a poorly functioning one, can make to team performance and the desire to do a bit extra for your colleagues and for the organization.

One executive explained how they loved working in one leadership team they were a part of. Why? Because they really helped each other out. If the executive (who led this particular team) was not around, the team would set up a call and discuss matters with each other. Then, when the executive was back – from holiday, for example, or from travelling on business – the team would let the executive know that they had talked about a particular problem, and what solution they arrived at. It's fantastic, says the executive, and exactly the behaviour that is encouraged.

On the other hand this person is also a member of another leadership team. Here the team culture is the complete opposite. 'It's dog eat dog. It's a shark tank. And it's just not a great place to be around. You want to get in and get out as quickly as possible. And it doesn't encourage any discretionary effort.'

Team Talk – Action Points

Most people belong to a number of teams at work. At the smallest level that might be the small projects team in their department, while at the other end of the scale they are part of the organization as a whole. Our research reveals that a strong driver of discretionary effort is identification with the teams that you belong to. Remember though that team identification is not the same as being friends with everyone on your team. It's a common misconception that you need to be friends with your team if you are going to work together well. But that is not the case. It is always possible that there will be some people with whom you click and enjoy working with, but others that you struggle to get along with. This should not prevent people identifying with their team.

In some organizations and some teams, team identification will happen naturally. However, in many cases a little extra effort will be required to help the process of team identification along. Fortunately, there are a few simple techniques and interventions that can be adopted to help reinforce the process of team identification.

1. Establish the 'next 100 days' meetings

Many teams or groups meet weekly or monthly and annually, these are all good meeting structures to have in place. The 100 day meetings however can be a bit different. By meeting every 100 days teams can set stretching goals and have time to implement them. The format of these can be a bit different too; some process or work stuff followed by some creative and ideas generating elements. A chance to think differently, and put thoughts or ideas forward which otherwise would not find a voice, can work well. Other ideas include a guest speaker or input from an outside source, industry specialist or member of the team with a different perspective or activity outside work.

By keeping these meetings scheduled at every 100 days they move throughout the year and provide at least three key moments for people to look forward to.

2. Encourage initiations and team rituals

These are shared 'rights of passage' as part of becoming a member of the team. Note that I am definitely not talking about 'hazing' and other initiations which are painful, unpleasant or humiliating. One idea on a team away day was to get each member of the team to talk for one minute about something outside of work which is important to them. This worked so well for a team that I worked with that they continued it as new people joined – it allowed team members to see something of the person behind the job title.

The team rituals can be as simple as someone bringing cakes in on their own birthday or ringing a bell in a shared office when a sale is made. Other rituals can be more complex, or indeed more subtle; however, the idea of a ritual demonstrates our commitment to the team and our rightful place in it.

Some work teams may even have their own branded clothing – with the company logo on one part of the clothing, and an individual team logo designed by the team elsewhere.

3. Conference calls – keep them focused and have a theme

For teams who work across big areas, or even countries, conference calling and Skype can be the main form of communication. Calls which go on too long and include too many topics for business are demotivating and time wasting. More regular calls, that are shorter in length, work better in many circumstances.

The idea behind having a theme is to be clear what the call is about and to allow for some different ways of working to stimulate interest and ideas. Themes could include:

* New Ideas – things we've never thought of;
* One Minute Moan – all team members have one minute to get stuff off their chests;
* Q Storm – question storm, to allow people to ask all the questions on a topic they'd like to get answers for;
* Big Me Up – a positive feedback session where all members need to offer good stuff to their colleagues;

- Challenges and Requests – all members share their biggest challenge and state what would be the most help right now. Others listen and respond outside the call if they think they can help.

4. Create a hall of fame or team zone

This is a place people associate with their team, a base to relax or meet or a wall with a notice board exclusively for team business/pleasure. It can help teams to associate with each other. A hall of fame is a collection of photos of team members doing great work stuff or interesting social stuff, allowing the team to see more of each other and to celebrate each other's successes.

5. Who is on my team?

Remember that one individual may well belong to many different teams. At any one time they may be part of a small project team, a product or service line, a business function, a business unit, a region, the organization as a whole. It may not be possible for each individual to identify with each team equally. However, they should still understand the different teams that they are a part of and feel some sense of belonging to each. At the same time, though, there may be conflicts of interests and objectives between the different teams, and these will need to be managed carefully if everyone is to stay aligned to the overall goals of the organization.

8. THE IMPORTANCE OF TRUST

'Trust men and they will be true to you; treat them greatly, and they will show themselves great.'

Ralph Waldo Emerson

L earning about trust is an essential part of growing up. We learn who to trust and who not to trust – "don't trust strangers" we are told as young children, for example. We discover when to trust and when not to trust. Every time we sit behind a steering wheel, we are about to take on trust, the competence of hundreds, if not thousands, of other road users and pedestrians. We find out what it takes to undermine trust, and what it feels like to have our trust broken.

For some people, trust is not just a 'nice to have', but a critical component of their activities. I know many mountaineers and rock climbers, for example, and have also climbed myself. For these people trust is an essential part of what they do – trust in themselves, trust in their equipment and trust in their climbing partners.

Society could not function without trust, and business is the same. For centuries, people have sealed business deals on nothing more than a handshake and trust. Take my business. As a speaker I focus much of my energy in developing a trusting relationship with my clients. That means I must deliver on a number of different levels.

At a basic level I'll turn up on time, or if not I'll be early. It's quite incredible how often speakers turn up with minutes to spare or are late. Quite understandably this puts the conference organizers into a spin as they try and reorganize their schedule. My clients also hope that I will follow the brief that I have been given and will engage with their delegates, showing interest in their world and relating to it in my presentation.

They also trust that I will do more than the bare minimum. Speakers who turn up, deliver a lacklustre presentation, and then leave at the earliest possible moment, leave a bad taste in the mouth. Commitments permitting I will always spend as much time with the delegates as I can. To me, it's customer service.

All of this means I have a trusting relationship with my clients, but the biggest benefit occurs after I have left the event and the delegates are back at work. The client then recommends me to their contacts. They are willing to put their own reputation on the line because they believe and trust that I will deliver again for others.

Trust is clearly an important factor in that organization–supplier, or organization–customer relationship, but it is also vital for the effective operation of the organization. You need to be able to trust your colleagues, and to trust your boss.

On the 5 August 2010, the miners at the San José copper and gold mine in Chile started their shift, just as they had countless times before. But a few hours later, following a major cave-in, the 33 men, or 'Los 33' as they became known, became trapped 2300 feet below ground, in the dark prison that was to be their home for the next 69 days.

Step forward Luis Urzúa, the shift boss; a man with the reputation for protecting and caring for his team. It was Urzúa who took on the responsibility of leading the miners through such a trying time. It took several hours for the dust to eventually settle, and although some men were optimistic that they might be rescued within a couple of days, Urzúa thought differently, and so he began to focus the men's minds on surviving this ordeal.

Each miner was given a specific job and Urzúa organized work shifts, which kept everyone busy, improved their living conditions and emphasized that individual's importance to the group. To avoid any conflict on ration distribution he ensured that everyone ate their one teaspoon of tuna and a half-glass of milk at the same time, every 48 hours.

When the rescue team first made voice contact with the miners, Urzúa responded: 'It's been a bit of a long shift'. He combined humour with courage and the responsibility of leadership. When the men were finally rescued, after 70 long days imprisoned beneath the Atacama desert, Urzúa was the last man out. Although it was the surface rescue team that eventually got the miners out, their survival was aided by Urzúa's leadership. He gave his men hope and direction and, in return, they gave him the help he needed to keep them alive. And that relationship was founded on trust.

Trust and discretionary effort

Our research shows that trust is an important driver of discretionary effort. Here I am referring to trust on several levels. For example, it refers to the extent to which an individual is willing to trust the senior management of the organization, and other individuals including fellow team members, or their leader. It also refers to whether someone is more or less willing to ascribe good intentions to – and have confidence in – the words and actions of other people in the company.

When I say leader, people might naturally focus on the CEO, but it is also about your immediate boss, and every other leader in the organization. In the most basic terms if you do not trust your leaders why would you provide discretionary effort? Of course, people do things for personal reasons or more altruistic reasons, but it is unlikely that someone will consistently provide discretionary effort if they do not believe that their leaders will recognize or reward that extra effort. The more that the organization, and individuals within that organization, engender trust the more likely it is that someone within that organization will go the extra mile.

Of course, the issue of trust extends beyond the internal workings of the organization. Trust also concerns how the organization is perceived. Its brand and reputation. If an organization suffers a loss of reputation, it may also lose the trust of its stakeholders, the customers, suppliers and the employees. And this can then affect levels of discretionary effort.

Take, for example, a senior director questioning the quality of the company's goods, as Gerald Ratner, Chief Executive of the jewellers, the Ratner Group, famously did; or a company struggling to handle a crisis, as BP did with the Deepwater Horizon oil spill. Any event that dents the reputation of the organization is likely to have a knock-on effect on discretionary effort.

Why should I trust you?

Trust has always been important in organizational life, but it has become particularly relevant in recent years because of developments in both the corporate world and more generally in society. Political scandals, such as the misuse of expenses by politicians in the UK, have undermined the public's trust in the government. The undermining of confidence in the political class that such scandals create feeds through to a lower turnout of voters in elections. Voting after all is about discretionary effort. And if people don't trust politicians as a whole, then they can't be bothered to vote for them.

The actions of politicians in undermining trust have been compounded by corporate scandals: both those that touch on the workings of government, such as the News International phone hacking scandal; and those that merely help tip the world into recession and austerity, such as the credit crunch and banking crisis. Add product problems such as the recent PIP breast implant crisis, where sub grade materials were improperly used for medical operations, or the metal-on-metal hip implant problems that emerged in 2010, and issues of trust seem more relevant than ever. If anything we are facing a crisis of trust.

Trust is just as important at work. Trust impacts on the working lives of employees in many ways. If the management abuses the trust of its employees by taking excessive risks with the future of the company, for example, it can cost employees their livelihoods. If a leader lets down their team, particularly if they do so frequently, it is likely to adversely affect team performance. If an individual finds that their confidence in their teammates is misplaced, that resulting lack of trust will affect that individual's performance.

Trust can make the difference between success and failure. One manager explained how, after a company reorganization, they inherited one particular employee who had once been a high performer tipped for career success. Subsequently, however, standards seemed to have slipped, leading to a low performance rating from a previous manager.

The new manager was keen to find out why this particular individual had underperformed. As it turned out, there were very good personal reasons that were affecting this employee's performance. The trouble was that they didn't trust their previous manager sufficiently to tell that manager their problems

In fact, the individual in question felt that they were in the wrong job, but didn't feel comfortable sharing that information with their leaders. They took on responsibilities and things for which they were not well-suited, struggled, and underperformed. However, once this person had confided in a new manager, it was fairly easy to make some adjustments to the job role and assignments. Before long the person became a high performer again. So there they were, at risk of losing their job and leaving the company. Yet all it took was a sufficiently strong bond of trust, between manager and employee, to turn the situation around. The employee got back on track, and once again was able to make a significant contribution to the company.

Drivers in Action: Trust

Fairness, Trust

'So it's being trustworthy. It's taking people at their word but, equally, it's showing that management is actually listening and they're interested in people's opinions and they're prepared to take decisions based on those opinions.

'We're building up trust with the staff and, although we may not always get it right, we do want to get it right and, increasingly, people start enjoying what they're doing and where they're working, and that really is the key to it. And if staff have got a smile on their face when they're dealing with a customer, then the customer will smile as well.'

A senior manager in the services industry

As the issue of trust has become a more prominent part of life recently, more organizations have begun to study trust, partly in an effort to understand what causes people to trust each other, and to trust organizations. There are various studies, books and papers on the subject. For the purposes of simplicity, however, I will focus on recent research by the Institute of Leadership and Management (ILM) in the UK.

Several years ago, the ILM began investigating the subject of trust in some depth. It constructed a model of trust and its constituent components and drivers, created a Trust Index, and has since conducted an annual trust survey of UK businesses together with an annual report on trust and associated issues.

ILM's six dimensions of trust

Given that trust is an important driver of discretionary effort it is worth exploring what builds trust in organizations. The ILM's research is a good place to start. The ILM offers a model of trust with six dimensions: ability, understanding, fairness, openness, integrity and consistency. Peter Chase was chairman at the ILM at the time – he has since moved on to become CEO of the CIPD – and I spoke to him about trust and the ILM's findings.

It is worth noting that some of these drivers, such as fairness, and knowledge and understanding of the employer (procedural justice and individualized consideration), are also direct drivers of discretionary effort.

This is very important. On the one hand it makes writing this chapter a particular challenge. When I spoke to people about trust they invariably discussed it in relation to the other drivers of discretionary effort. And, therefore, for the sake of avoiding repetition I have tended to use those comments to illustrate those particular drivers rather than the notion of trust. At the same time it highlights those interconnected nature of the discretionary effort drivers – and emphasizes the importance for organizations to address them together, where possible and not in isolation.

Ability
The first driver of trust, as identified by the ILM, is ability. Fundamentally, this relates to whether you believe a colleague or boss has the ability to perform the job that they are in.

It is about that unfortunately common experience at work when someone gives you instructions and you think: 'Hold on a minute, they don't know what they are talking about.

I don't know why they're telling me to do that because they can't even do it themselves.'

A lack of confidence in the ability of others can have a significant impact on performance. There is an analogy in football (soccer). When teammates don't believe in the ability of a fellow player, they don't pass to them. And so just that simple lack of confidence erodes collaboration and team performance as, effectively, the team plays with one player fewer than the opposition.

If you pay attention to the people around, you can see the same principle in operation at work. If people do not believe in the ability of their boss to do the job, for example, they may well only follow the leader's instructions reluctantly, if at all. Equally, if the team does not have confidence in the abilities of a particular team member they may not entrust them with certain tasks, or share information, or ask for the person's opinion.

Drivers in Action: Trust

Ability, Trust, Empowerment

'I learned fairly quickly that I'm a bit of a workaholic. I'll take more on than perhaps I think the new kid on the block is able to do. But quickly you should realize that is not your role. You are not going to be as effective as a leader, if you are doing everybody's job for them.

So at some point you've got to give it up. You've got to delegate. Personally, once I have the trust and confidence in the team or in the individual, I have found it very easy to do that.'

Senior executive in a global business services organization

There may also be a generational and cultural influence at work in relation to this dimension of trust. A culture of trust and respect is particularly strong in some countries, and with that an inherent belief in the wisdom of elders. In Japan, for example, it is likely that younger people will have confidence in the ability of older colleagues, because respect for the wisdom of elders is ingrained in the country's culture. That is true of other nations too. In the west, however, even if that respect once existed it has certainly been eroded. Research by the ILM and others, for example, suggests that Generation Y are far less likely to take the ability of older colleagues for granted.

As Peter Cheese notes: chairman of the ILM notes: 'I think young people here today say, "just because you're my elder, or you're sat in a position that is senior to me, doesn't mean to say that you instantly command my respect or that I instantly trust you just by virtue of the fact that you're older or in that position. You have got to earn that respect." I think we are more demanding of people in any position of authority, to earn our respect, and demonstrate that they have the ability to do the job.'

Understanding

The second driver of trust is understanding. This links strongly with the concept of individualized consideration, which we discuss at length in Chapter 4. Here we are talking about managers having a good knowledge and understanding of their employees. There are many ways that organizations can improve their performance with regards to individualized consideration, whether that is the ways in which they find out what really motivates employees, or how they go about rewarding employees in ways that make them feel special.

With trust, however, there is a particular emphasis on understanding the employee's role and responsibilities. Ultimately, you are more likely to trust someone, who not only appears to know what they are doing, but also appears to have a clear understanding of what you are meant to be doing, and is able to explain how that contributes to the organization's overall objectives.

Fairness and openness

Another two components of trust identified by the ILM's research, fairness and openness, appear to be closely related to each other and to the discretionary effort driver procedural justice.

Fairness is about behaving fairly and showing concern for the welfare of the employees. If people believe that their boss is treating them fairly in relation to the other employees they are more likely to trust their boss. This links with aspects of work such as performance evaluation, reward and recognition, and career progression.

For example, performance management systems and the promotion process are often opaque. Even where there has been more visibility, engrained organizational habits such as tenure-based promotion often seem manifestly unfair in a business world where talent is meant to be of paramount importance and rewarded accordingly.

As I outlined in Chapter 6 (Fair's Fair) greater openness and transparency help to create a sense of fairness, and so build trust. Of course there will still be limits to how open organizations are. However, it is surprising how far it is possible to go. As we have seen in some Nordic countries, for example, there are companies that publish people's salary grades. And today's organizations are far more willing to publish information on non-financial information, such as corporate social responsibility performance and sustainability related data.

The commitment to openness should run throughout the organization, with the relationship between staff and externally with customers and other stakeholders in the value chain. As one manager expressed it: 'You have got to try your best to produce and drive forward a culture where people are able to say, "yes, this company is honest, the leadership is honest, we feel open and transparent with each other."

'And this should extend to your clients as well. In the past there have been a couple of instances where we have been in situations with clients where some of our staff have felt uncomfortable. Perhaps because we over promised, and we were in danger of under delivering, for example. So you've got to make sure you don't get into those situations.'

Openness should apply to leadership too. There are many ways that leaders are able to communicate with people in the organization. Whereas in the past it might have been written memos, Post-it notes, speeches to a mass audience, now many leaders and managers will use social media, such as blogs, Twitter, or Facebook, to communicate with their teams and the organization.

In an age where there are significant generational differences in attitudes towards privacy, this kind of openness is almost expected. Social media allows leaders to express their beliefs and values to a wider audience. It helps them to convey a sense of them as a real person, and as an individual, which in turn helps to demonstrate authenticity.

'It's vitally important that an organization has open communications. There are things we will talk about at the senior leadership team which for various reasons, you can't share, but there's absolutely no reason why you can't share the rest of the conversation. Any senior leadership team meeting is reported to everybody in the company, so everybody knows what's going on.

'We have a senior leadership team meeting every two weeks, and within a day a full note of the meeting has been put out. So people know what we've been talking about, what we've been doing. I think it matters to people that you trust them enough to share with them what's happening; I think it is part of building that sense of we're all part of one team.'

Remember, though, that communication is one of those things where different methods suit different people. Some people listen well, some people prefer to see something written down. So it is both about openness, and about accepting that good communication has to be in all modes, from regular updates on email, to monthly WebEx staff updates.

Of course there are dangers too. Being open exposes organizations and individuals to greater scrutiny, both from within the organizations, and from external sources too. It is far easier for errors of judgment, and injudicious comments to find their way into the wider world where they form a permanent record widely available that can undermine trust and destroy reputations.

This is where the next component of trust becomes so important.

Consistency

The importance of consistency as a key element of trust is also confirmed by Rupert Younger, the founding director of the Oxford University Centre for Corporate Reputation based at Oxford University's Said Business School, co-founder of the RLM Finsbury Group, the global financial communications group, and an expert on reputation-related matters.

'Trust is built through regular interaction,' says Younger. 'It is quite difficult to build trust in a one-off event. If I meet you once and I happen to behave in a certain way, you don't necessarily trust me on that basis, because you have only seen me once. It starts to build a pattern of behaviour in your mind. But trust only works with repeated interactions. So the trust is lesser or greater depending on the depth and breadth of interaction that you have with your organization, and indeed with your team and your boss.'

For employees, trust in their colleagues and bosses is built through regular interaction which reveals consistent behaviour. I have seen the damage that can be done to trust when a manager exhibits a particular set of behaviours one day, and then another the next. Or when there is a boss who behaves in different ways depending on which team member they are dealing with. Each instance of inconsistent behaviour erodes trust. Perhaps they always defend one particular member of staff, regardless of whether that is justified or not, but never defend another.

It's worth remembering that consistency is only valuable when coupled with quality. One senior director for example, walks the floor at the same time every Friday – and gives nothing but positive feedback. Ten out of ten for consistency; three out of ten for management style.

Integrity
Consistency of behaviour is closely linked to integrity, the last of the six drivers of trust identified by ILM's research.

Some might take the position that integrity is something that is rooted in early development, and therefore cannot be fostered or coached in organizations or individuals. But many others including ILM's chairman Peter Cheese, others think it is both possible, and important to do so.

Authenticity is one facet of integrity at both the individual and organizational level. The actions of leaders need to back up their words. Similarly the values that the organization espouses need to be backed up by the way it treats its people. When managers talk about the corporate mission and values, they should visibly behave in ways that support the mission and values. This engenders trust in the organization, which then promotes the desired behaviours from employees, including discretionary effort. One executive who worked for a non-profit organization explained how the actions of some staff inspired discretionary effort in others.

'You have to win hearts and minds. In an organization like mine, which is a charitable one with a really strong mission to improve kids' lives through PE and sport, in a sense it's an easy sell for your staff. But for those staff who come to do day-to-day admin support, for example, who don't come as "missionaries," I suddenly find all of them volunteering on one of our camps at the weekend. And that is about winning over their hearts and minds, it's not about their job descriptions. And part of that is that they've got to buy the mission, whatever that mission is. The mission has to be so important, or they can understand its importance sufficiently, we're all part of one team'

Another aspect of integrity that is often overlooked is fallibility. As Cheese points out, corporate leaders make mistakes, and there is no shame in admitting that. 'It's very frustrating when mistakes are made but the boss won't admit to it. I don't care if you are the CEO of one of the largest organizations. You're a human being. You make mistakes. And I make mistakes and it helps me to trust you if I can see that you acknowledge and admit where you might not have done everything perfectly.'

Integrity as a driver of trust and thus discretionary effort also links to the idea of sacrificial leadership as a driver of discretionary effort. Take the P&G executive I mentioned in Chapter 5 who shared the results of his 360 review with his team. He did this to encourage greater openness amongst his team, and in doing so he also displayed he was a person of integrity.

Or as another executive observed: 'Sacrificial leadership is something where you are building an element of trust – I trust you to make decisions for the good of the organization. It is not about selfish and selfless acts – there will always be selfish and selfless motivations for action.'

'If you are going to inspire trust as a leader, you should lead for the right reasons. Your decisions must be leading in the right direction. People don't see that as though you're biasing your decisions to suit yourself.

'And it is those kinds of decisions that build trust for the good of the organization. That is a simple example, but a good example of how you shift from people taking actions only in their own interests to showing people that the organization is creating a structure that is going to allow a better way of making decisions that are in the interest of the right parties.'

Trust is a state of mind

Organizations can help to create an atmosphere of trust by focusing on the individual drivers of trust outlined above. In doing so, they will also be going some way to attending to the drivers of discretionary effort. But the organization can only do so much.

There is also the question of an individual's tendency to trust or mistrust people. Some of this inevitably stems from experiences as a child and growing up, which shape attitudes about trustworthiness as an adult. Different people have different approaches to the issue of trust. For many it is either a glass half empty or glass half full approach.

Perhaps the approach to take is that of one manager we spoke to who said: 'My thoughts on that are pretty simple. I will trust people until they give me a reason not to. I usually declare that right up front, as a management style. I tell people, I'm candid with them about it.'

Drivers in Action: Trust

Acknowledging Challenges

'The whole business of trust is that you have to understand, like you do when you teach or you coach, that sometimes the best way for people to learn is to get something wrong. You can't always stop things going wrong, maybe you can stop the big things going wrong by the way you manage things, but people are going to have to try and experiment, and the trust comes, not from people always getting it absolutely right, but people being honest about how they're doing.

'It's trust to say, "I tried that and it really didn't come off." Knowing that your boss isn't going to say, "well, you're an idiot, out the door," rather than, "let's have a think about that, and let's make sure we don't ever do that again."'

Head of a third sector organization

The importance of trust – Action Points

Trust is the big cornerstone of successful relationships. Like money, trust can take a long time to build up and a moment to lose. If, through the other chapters, I have provided you with the building blocks for discretionary effort then trust is the cement that holds them all together. Without it all your other hard work has been wasted and people won't go the extra mile for you. They might for the customer but they won't for you. Given the descriptions above about the elements of trust, what are the simple, actionable steps any manager can take to build up trust?

1. Behind every 'what' there is a 'why'

Knowing the reason behind what people do is a very important component of trust. When staff understand the reason for rules, the justification for your actions and the background behind change, it is much easier for them to see why you or the organization have done something. When people do not know things they fill in the gaps themselves – often with incorrect assumptions and suspicions. When you lead with total transparency, and have few or no secrets, you create much more fertile ground for trust to grow. Avoid assuming people know or understand your motives or reasons, always go further and explain yourself and ask the business or your line management to explain changes, decisions and initiatives and then cascade this information as accurately as you can.

2. Five simple rules

The following rules, if stuck to, will build and reinforce trust. They do not need a great deal of explaining, they are about doing.

1. Keep promises – only commit to what you are prepared to deliver on
2. Admit mistakes – put things right and own up to problems or mistakes
3. Talk straight – speaking the truth with sensitivity
4. Seek clarity – establish expectations at all times before acting
5. Trust others – the quickest route to generating trust is to open up and begin to trust others

3. Make a commitment to improve

The Relationship Map below plots the nature of your key and peripheral work relationships. Using the following guide, mark yourself in the middle and your colleagues/clients around you based on perceived proximity and quality of connection.

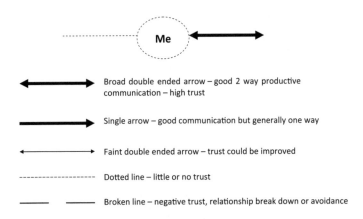

Now rate your trust levels 1–10 (1 being low and 10 being high) between you and others in the organization with whom you have to interact to do your daily business. Then, be bold, and ask them to rate the levels of trust they feel towards you.

Notice the differences and talk about how these scores could be improved.

4. No one is right all of the time

We do not get it right all of the time and some honesty around this is important. Telling others you value trust and you value their trust is a positive step towards improving trust. Explaining what you feel are your shortcomings, and that you would like feedback as appropriate to rebuild trust, helps people understand your perspective and begin to trust you.

This may require some tough conversations, however. For trust to build there needs to be a great deal of honesty, something that people can be very wary of. Being open, and totally clear about your intentions, helps people to realize that you are not keeping secrets, and using what they say against them.

9. NEXT STEPS

'The secret of success is constancy of purpose.'
Benjamin Disraeli British politician

The business case for discretionary effort

As I mentioned at the beginning of the book, one of the main reasons I became involved with the discretionary effort project, was due to the many conversations I had with executives as I travelled the world on my speaking engagements. They sensed that colleagues were willing to go the extra mile in contributing towards to the goals of the organization, but weren't sure of the best way to help them get there. It was finding that elusive key to unlock the full potential of employees.

As I began to find out more about discretionary effort, many people, both before, during, and after the research was conducted, told me their stories of how discretionary effort had helped their organization in different situations.

The anecdotal evidence for the importance of discretionary effort, and the role that it can play in an organization's success, appeared overwhelming. But anecdotal evidence doesn't always carry much weight with the decision makers in organizations. If you want to take culture changing action, obtain funding for projects and initiatives, alter some of the fundamental ways that people behave, shape training and development, introduce new hiring criteria, adapt leadership approaches, then you are likely to need more than anecdotal evidence to support your case.

Fortunately, the research we did also revealed some hard, objective evidence to support the case for encouraging discretionary effort. The team tested discretionary effort to see if it correlated with a number of important and commonly used performance metrics. The results were particularly encouraging and exciting. As the team examined the research data it became clear that an increase in discretionary effort positively correlated with a better score for a basket of metrics, many relating to performance.

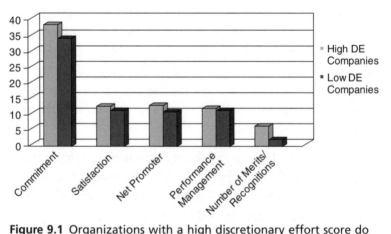

Figure 9.1 Organizations with a high discretionary effort score do better than those with a low discretionary effort score across a number of performance metrics

The metrics that the team used will be familiar to anyone involved in organizational or team performance assessment. They included: group cohesiveness; net promoter score; sick days and paid vacation; the quality of performance; performance management; recent bonuses, merits, and recognition; commitment; and job satisfaction. The higher the discretionary effort score that an organization gained, for example, the less likely it was that that employees would take fake sick days, the higher the self-reported performance scores of employees, and the greater the formal recognition of those employees in the workplace.

Discretionary effort in your organization

The link between better discretionary effort scores and improved performance, across a range of important metrics, just reinforces the case for making an organization a more discretionary effort friendly place to work. And I have explained the best way to do this is by focusing on the relevant aspects of organizational life.

By now, hopefully, you will have a good understanding of what discretionary effort is, and the six main drivers that have a powerful impact on discretionary effort. You may also have an instinctive feel for how your organization performs across these critical business challenges.

* **Autonomy and empowerment:** Are employees empowered to take decisions on their own in the interests of the organization, for example? Or are they constrained and micromanaged with little room for using their initiative and innovative talents?

- **Individualized consideration:** Do leaders in the organization bother to find out what makes their team members tick? Do they care about people as individuals? Is reward targeted to personal motivation? Is leadership visible, or is it hidden away?

- **Self-sacrificial leadership:** Are the managers and leaders just looking out for themselves and their own careers, or do they put the interests of others first? Does an ethos of service run right through the organization? Is performance assessed on a team, as well as an individual basis?

- **Procedural justice:** Do you work in an organization that believes in fairness, openness and transparency? Do promotions go to the best candidates or to favourites? Are people who don't pull their weight dealt with, or is poor performance tolerated in some cases? Is justice done, and seen to be done? Do structures like virtual teams or matrix management complicate team identification in your organization?

- **Team identification:** Is there a sense of belonging, whether that is to teams, business units or the organization? Do people understand the role that they play in their team? Is knowledge readily shared, and collaboration and cooperation embraced? Or are people secretive and protective over information?

- **Trust:** Do you trust your boss? Do they trust you? Do you both trust the company? Is the behaviour of leaders in the organization likely to build trust? Are they behaving consistently? Do team members believe that their leader is competent? Would employees say that behaving with integrity was important to the organization?

Knowing the answers to these kinds of questions is the first step in the process of creating a better environment for discretionary effort. Take a moment to reflect on how well your team or company might score if it was tested across some of these drivers. Where do you think your people are strong and where might they be performing less well. Start to explain the discretionary effort concept and its drivers to people in the organization and consider the responses? If you think that there are gaps between where you are and where you should be, the next step is to consider assessing performance across the drivers in a more rigorous way.

The benefits of improving the drivers for discretionary effort appear almost irrefutable. In the past the challenge has been not knowing what factors feed into discretionary effort, or how to measure whether or not a firm is performing on these factors. Now, however, organizations are able to complete the survey devised as part of the research that formed the basis of this book.

The survey

Two surveys have been created. One is a 'light' version that can provide a snapshot of businesses capabilities and areas for improvement that, with a little guidance, can form the basis for any developmental strategy. The second survey provides more depth, allowing firms to assess their performance across the drivers of discretionary effort in some detail.

The survey covers the five broad areas of: discretionary effort; work engagement; leadership; organization environment; and personality. In doing so it looks at the drivers discussed in Chapters 3–8: autonomy, empowerment, structure and procedure, self-sacrificing, leadership, individualized consideration, trustworthiness, and team identification.

At the same time it also looks at a number of other drivers: dedication, vigour, absorption, agreeableness, clarity, conscientiousness, and charisma.

Before taking the survey it is also important for the organization to consider what its current business priorities are. So, for example, I worked with a global software company that wanted to put extraordinary customer service at the heart of all that it did. The challenge was to make this feel relevant for all of their staff regardless of whether they came into contact with a customer or not.

The solution, from a developmental point of view, was to focus on empowerment. Their people had to base all their decisions on whether or not they made a positive impact on the customer. To make that a cultural shift the team leaders had to empower them. So this intervention focused on a driver of discretionary effort, but in a way that was most relevant to the business in question.

Completing the survey will provide the organizations with some hard data to compare to the anecdotal evidence coming back from the employees, customers and other stakeholders. The next stage is to look at key areas for improvement. Completing the survey for your team, department of organization could also provide the data required to help make a case for more resources or funds to support a change initiative.

The Discretionary Effort Challenge

Training, Development and Support

Organizations should make sure that they provide adequate training, development and support alongside any discretionary effort initiative.

For example, survey results may reveal a lack of autonomy within the workforce that the organization decides to address, by empowering its people and offering greater decision making freedom. However, simply handing over greater authority and responsibility without offering adequate support and training to manage the transition, is likely to lead to failure as individuals are exposed beyond their initial comfort zones and abilities.

It is the same for the other drivers. Leaders will struggle to develop self-sacrificing abilities as I have described them without first having a clear understanding of what it means to be a leader. Team identification won't happen in a meaningful way unless the team leaders understand the foundations of team building.

So, adequate provision of training, development and support, whether that is sourced internally or from an external provider, is essential.

Top down, bottom up

Not everyone has the budget to hire external consultants to support them with training and development. Or indeed you may feel you are more than capable of tackling some of the issues and challenges we have covered in the book. If so, great, go for it!

However, you may want to consider consulting with someone that has an in-depth understanding of discretionary effort, behavioural development and the broader employee engagement picture.

The survey provides a detailed analysis of the key elements of discretionary effort. From this a firm can build a mental picture of motivation and morale in its company and how likely it is for its people to 'go the extra mile'.

We know that a significant part of discretionary effort relates to leadership behaviours, and this is an excellent place to start.

A top down, bottom up, inside out approach is essential! By this I mean that a coordinated series of interventions, co-designed by the managers and staff looking at the survey scores and building a thorough approach will get the best results.

Stage one should be an interpretive meeting with a discretionary effort experienced coach. Next, a series of focus groups and discussion meetings to share the results of the survey with the staff will help to keep the topic alive, and bring it to people's attention. People will remember completing the questionnaire and these meetings will provide continuity.

This then gives the staff the opportunity to contribute to the improvement of the discretionary effort environment and be a part of the design of any development. It is hoped that by creating a better environment for discretionary effort it will discourage organizations from trying to implement measures that deliberately force additional effort and improved performance in ways which are detrimental to the workforce well being in the long run. Instead the organizations should be able to create the conditions for the employees to want to do more, and perform better.

Overcoming barriers
The benefits of maximizing the discretionary effort given by your employees are clearly apparent. However, it is important to consider how a company's push towards discretionary effort will be perceived. Plans to enhance a team's ability to deliver will, of course, be welcomed with open arms by the team leaders but what about their teams?

Managers are likely to encounter the classic human response to change – people tend to avoid change rather than seek it out. Inclusion and information allow people to see what is behind the changes and to understand how working on discretionary effort can help. Having discretionary effort coaches throughout the business keeps the topic alive, and enables people to have a 'go to' person to whom they can take any concerns.

At all times the emphasis must be on creating better, more enjoyable, workplace environments where people choose to go the extra mile, be that for their team mates, their customers, or for the business in a more general sense. The choice must be theirs. If people are being coerced then the benefits will be lost.

Key success points

There are some key pointers to overall success with a discretionary effort intervention.

- **Good communication:** There is a critical need to communicate what a discretionary effort project means to the different levels within the business. Fundamentally it means better work environments and practices for the workers and more trusting, open, honest and empowering behaviours from the team leaders.
- **Personal Responsibility:** Team leaders need to understand that it is their behaviours that are the most crucial ingredient in creating environments where people choose to freely give discretionary effort. They need to take personal responsibility to deliver day-to-day on any cultural change programme with a discretionary effort focus.
- **Senior management buy-in:** As with all interventions, senior management buy-in is crucial. Why change your behaviour and sign up for cultural change when your leadership team clearly doesn't? Senior management needs to understand the impact a discretionary effort project

could have on the bottom line, and they need to understand how they will be asking their people to behave. It
is notoriously difficult to get senior management to attend
training, but the positive impact on them understanding
and living by the principles contained within the six drivers
would ripple through the organization.

- **DE champions:** A step towards embedding discretionary
  effort principles into all areas of a business is to make them
  integral to staff development and recognition. A powerful
  way to generate appropriate behaviours is to recognize
  them either formally or informally. Some may say that
  in doing so people will start to behave in a certain way, in
  expectation of reward, and therefore the actions are not
  discretionary effort. But what I am suggesting here is not
  that everyone receives a bonus for a good deed or positive
  action. Rather that managers and leaders occasionally highlight something and, most importantly, remember to say
  thank you or well done every now and then.

Other actions that can be useful include open space sessions
where people can come and learn about the drivers of discretionary effort, what they mean, and how they can help
them improve their performance. Also useful are small con-
ferences in break times and public spaces in the company,
which keep the message alive and explain the issues. Follow
these by inviting key players, including discretionary effort
champions, to development meetings where they contribute
to any initiative.

Planting seeds
In writing this final chapter I realized that my own views
on discretionary effort have evolved considerably over time.

What started as a chance conversation became an intellectual challenge and has led to my passionate belief that better workplace environments can be created which benefit both employee and employer alike.

With hindsight, discretionary effort has been a central thread throughout all of the successes I have enjoyed, whether sporting, business or charitable in nature. When I set up my consulting business SladenWoods, I did so with the deep desire to help organizations and people achieve their potential in the world – to be brilliant at something. That desire was also reflected in my autobiographical and motivational book *Personal Best*. What I have captured in this book, I hope, is how organizations can focus on discretionary effort as a way to help achieve their visions and become brilliant in whatever they do.

In its full form, and at its best, the drive to create a discretionary effort environment can become a movement within an organization – a workplace revolution to liberate employees, allow them to achieve personal fulfillment through work, and enable them to contribute to their maximum.

The people that work in your organization have far more potential to contribute to the organization than you can possibly imagine. No matter what your position or role is, you can help your organization to unlock that potential. You have made a start by reading this book. Now try telling others about the power of discretionary effort.

Why wouldn't anyone want to create an environment in which discretionary effort is able to flourish? Isn't that the kind of organization that we would all want to be a part of?

I began this book with a small example of how I had encountered discretionary effort in my everyday life. It was just one small interaction, out of the hundreds of daily interactions, the thousands of weekly interactions, the millions of interactions we engage in over a lifetime. It was only a small fragment of my work life experience, yet it made a difference. It mattered to me. And it changed my perceptions of another business – in a good way.

It is fitting, then, that I finish this book with another example of how one person's discretionary effort has touched my life in a small but meaningful way.

My wife and I both enjoy spending time outside and so, with spring poised to burst into life, we decided to pay a visit to a garden centre. There were a couple to choose from locally, and being new to the area we picked a small one that had not been open for that long.

We sauntered around, deciding what would enhance the plants we already had at home. Eventually we came across a pair of hornbeam trees that had been grown together to form an arch almost 10 feet tall. For my wife it was love at first sight, and I knew better than to disagree.

'I'd intended to use them as an entrance to the nursery once the building work is completed, but if you like them . . .' Steven the owner said.

We settled on a price and, as they were so big, he offered to deliver them on his day off. True to his word he arrived the following Saturday morning with the two trees just about fitting into the back of his van. The trees were deceptively heavy, so it took some time for Steven and I to manoeuvre them into place. I'd expected him to simply drop the trees off and go and enjoy the rest of his day, but he stayed and helped me get them into the ground, which took almost three hours. He wanted us to be happy with where they were and how they looked. He even spent some time pruning them.

We certainly hadn't expected him to do this, especially on his one day off of the week, but we did very much appreciate it and, if at all possible, will never buy anything from any other garden centre again.

Now it is time for you to plant the seeds of discretionary effort in your organization.

ACKNOWLEDGEMENTS

Firstly, I would like to say thank you to Holly Bennion and her team at Wiley for their understanding, patience and help, from proposal to print. In Particular Jenny Ng who knows this book inside out and backwards.

I am also indebted to all those individuals and organizations that have helped me along the way; whether that was through inspiring conversation or discussions, or more formally with the quantitative and qualitative discretionary effort research.

They include Barclays, Bruntwood, BSkyB, Cafcass, Ceridian, Credit Suisse, Deloitte, Department for Work & Pensions, DX Group, ESurv, Genzyme, GSK, HBOS, IBM, InterContinental Hotel Group, jetBlue, Johnson & Johnson, JW Lees, Kraft, Lego, Lloyds TSB, LV=, Merton Priory Homes, Microsoft, O2, Ossur, Pepsico, Pfizer, Procter & Gamble, RBS, Remploy, Sage, Sainsburys, Southgate College, Tesco, Univar, Virgin Media, Visa International, Volvo, West Kent Housing Association, Youth Sport Trust and UK Power Networks.

A special mention must go to Dr Chris Rotolo and his research team, Na Hyun Kim, Kai Zhou and Gabriel Hui, at New York University's Department of Organizational

Psychology. They helped to clarify my initial musings and provided their academic insights.

From the outset I have wanted to produce something that, in the right hands, will have a positive impact in the workplace. Richard Colley and the SladenWoods network have enabled us to do this and, in particular, thanks must go to Piers Carter whose passion and insight as to how best develop practical interventions has been invaluable.

Finally my writing partner, and friend, Steve Coomber has shown considerable fortitude to help move this from the kernel of an idea, via the research, to the completion of this book.

Everyone involved in this project has, at some point, gone above and beyond the call of duty, and I am deeply grateful.

Thank you.

Borrowed items 30/06/2017 08:23
XXXXXX 119

Item Title	Due Date
Beyond the gateway to the vague from john m	20/06/2017
Kidnapped: the adventures of David Balfour in th	20/06/2017
Last of the Mohicans: penguin readers activity p	20/06/2017

Indicates items borrowed today
Thankyou for using this unit

READING LIST

A list of some of the academic papers produced during the literature review phase by the research team.

Cohen-Charash, Y., & Spector, P.E. (2001). The role of justice in organizations: A meta-analysis. *Organizational Behaviour and Human Decision Processes*, 86, 278–321

Bateman, T.S., & Organ, D.W. (1983). Job satisfaction and the good soldier: The relationship between affect and employee 'citizenship.' *Academy of Management Journal*, 26(4), 587–595

Bhattacharya, C.B., Rao, H., & Glynn, M.A. (1995). Understanding the bond of identification: an investigation of its correlates among art museum members. *Journal of Marketing*, Vol. 59, October, pp. 46–57

Blader, S., & Tyler, T.R. (2003). Testing the four component model of procedural justice. *Personality and Social Psychology Bulletin*, 29, 747–758

Blader, S., & Tyler, T.R., (2003). The four component model of procedural justice. *Human Resource Management Review*, 13, 107–126

Blader, S.L., & Tyler, T.R. (2009). Testing & extending the Group Engagement Model: Linkages between social identity, procedural justice, economic outcomes and extra role behaviour. *Journal of Applied Psychology*. Vol. 94, No. 2, 445–464

Bolino, M.C. (1999). Citizenship and impression management: Good soldiers or good actors? *Academy of Management Review*, 24, 82–98

Brief, A.P., & Motowildo, S.J. (1986). Prosocial Organizational Behaviours. *The Academy of Management Review*. 11(4), 710–725

Cappelli, P., & Rogovsky, N. (1994). New Work Systems and Skill Requirements. *International Labour Review*, Geneva: ILO, no.2, pp. 205–220, (in English, French and Spanish)

Choi, Y., & Mai-Dalton, R.R. (1999). The model of followers' responses to self-sacrificial leadership: An empirical test. *The Leadership Quarterly*, 10, 397–421

Choi, Y., & Mai-Dalton, R.R. (1998). On the leadership function of self-sacrifice. *The Leadership Quarterly*, 9, 475–501

Colquitt, J.A., Conlon, D.E., Wesson, M.J., Porter, C.O.L.H., & Ng, K.Y. (2001). Justice at the millennium: A meta-analytic review of 25 years of organizational justice research. *Journal of Applied Psychology*, 86, 425–445

Conte, J.M., Dean, M.A., Ringenbach, K.L., Moran, S.K., & Landy, F.L. (2005). The relationship between work attitudes and job analysis ratings: Do task rating scale type and task discretion matter? *Human Performance*, 18, 1–21

Cook, J., & Wall, T.D. (1980). New work attitude measures of trust, organizational commitment and personal need non-fulfilment. *Journal of Occupational Psychology*, 53, 39–52

Coyle-Shapiro, J.A-M., & Conway, N. (2005). Exchange relationships: examining psychological contracts and perceived organizational support. *Journal of applied psychology*, 90(4), 774–781

De Cremer, D., & van Knippenberg, D. (2004). Leader self-sacrifice and leadership effectiveness: The moderating role of leader self-confidence. *Organizational Behaviour and Human Decision Processes*, 95, 140

De Cremer, D., Mayer, D.M., Schouten, B.C., Bardes, M., & van Dijke, M. (2009). When does self-sacrificial leadership *motivate prosocial behaviour: It depends on followers' prevention focus. Journal of Applied Psychology,* 94, 887–899

Gagné, M. (2003). The role of autonomy support and autonomy orientation in prosocial behaviour engagement. *Motivation and Emotion,* 27, 199–223

Gagné, M., & Deci, E.L. (2005). Self-determination theory and work motivation. *Journal of Organizational Behaviour,* 26, 331–362

Gouldner, A. (1960). The Norm of Reciprocity: A Preliminary Statement. *American Sociological Review* 25, 161–178

Hoffman, M.L. (1981). Is Altruism a part of human nature? *Journal of Personality and. Social Psychology.* Vol 40

Ilies R., Spitzmuller M., Fulmer I.S., & Johnson M.D. (Jul 2009). Personality and citizenship behaviour: the mediating role of job satisfaction. *Journal of Applied Psychology,* Volume 94 Issue: 4 pp.945–959

In Rushton J.P., & Sorrentino, R.M. (1981) (Eds.), *Altruism and helping behaviour: Social, personality, and developmental perspectives:* 251–266. Hillsdale, NJ: Erlbaum

Korsgaard, M.A., Meglino, B.M., & Lester, S.W. (1997). Beyond helping: Do other-oriented values have broader implications in organizations? *Journal of Applied Psychology,* 82, 160–177

Law, S.K., Wong, C., & Chen, X.Z. (2005). The construct of organizational citizenship behaviour: Should we analyze after we have conceptualized? In D.L. Turnipseed (Ed.), *Handbook of organizational citizenship behaviour* (pp. 47–65). New York: Nova Science Publishers

Lind, A.E., & Tyler, T.R. (1988). *The Social Psychology of Procedural Justice,* New York: Plenum Press

Lloyd, R. (2008). Discretionary effort and the performance domain. *The Australian and New Zealand Journal of Organisational Psychology,* 1, 22–34

Macey, W.H., & Schneider, B. (2008). The Meaning of Employee Engagement. *Industrial and Organizational Psychology,* 1, 3–30

Moorman, R., & Byrne, Z.S. (2005). What is the Role of Justice in Promoting Organizational Citizenship Behaviour?, in J. Greenberg and J.A. Colquitt (Eds.). *Handbook of Organizational Justice: Fundamental Questions about Fairness in the Workplace* (pp. 355–382). Mahwah, NJ: Lawrence Erlbaum Associates

Morgeson, F.P., Delaney-Klinger, K.A., & Hemingway, M.A. (2005). The importance of job autonomy, cognitive ability, and job-related skill for predicting role breadth and job performance. *Journal of Applied Psychology*, 90, 399–406

Morris, L. (April 1996). Employees not Encouraged to go the Extra Mile. *Training & Development, Alexandria, VA*

O'Reilly, C., & Chatman, J. (1986). Organizational commitment and psychological attachment: The effects of compliance, identification, and internalization on prosocial behaviour. *Journal of Applied Psychology*, 71, 492–499

Organ, D.W. (1988). *Organizational Citizenship behaviour: The good soldier syndrome.* Lexington, MA: Lexington Books

Organ, D.W., & Ryan, K. (1995). A meta-analytic review of attitudinal and dispositional predictors of organizational citizenship behaviour. *Personnel Psychology*, 48(4), 775–802

Organ, D.W., Podsakoff, P.M., & MacKenzie S.P. (2006). *Organizational citizenship behaviour: Its nature, antecedents, and consequences.* London: Sage Publications

Parker, S.K. (1998). Role breadth self-efficacy: Relationship with work enrichment and other organisational practices. *Journal of Applied Psychology*, 83, 835–852

Parker, S.K., & Axtell, C.M. (2001). Seeing another viewpoint: Antecedents and outcomes of employee perspective taking. *Academy of Management Journal*, 44, 1085–1100

Perry, J.L., & Hondeghem, A. (2008). *Motivation in public management: The call of public service.* New York: Oxford University Press

Podsakoff, P.M., MacKenzie, S.B., Moorman, R.H., & Fetter, R. (1990). Transformational leader behaviours and their effects on followers' trust in leader, satisfaction, and organizational citizenship behaviours. *The Leadership Quarterly*, 1(2), 107–142

Rioux, S.M., & Penner, L.A. (2001). The causes of organizational citizenship behaviour: a motivational analysis. *Journal of Applied Psychology*, 86, 1306–1314

Rhoades, L., & Eisenberger, R. (2002). Perceived organizational support: A review of the literature. *Journal of Applied Psychology*, 87, 698–714

Roberts, B.W., Chernyshenko, O.S., Stark, S., & Goldberg, L.R. (2005). The structure of conscientiousness: An empirical investigation based on seven major personality questionnaires. *Personnel Psychology*, 58, 103–139

Shamir, B. (1991). Meaning, self and motivation in organizations. *Organization Studies*, 12, 405–424

Smith, C.A., Organ, D.W., & Near, J.P. (1983). Organizational citizenship behaviour: Its nature and antecedents. *Journal of Applied Psychology*, 68, 655–663

Tyler, T.R., & Blader, S. (2006). Can businesses effectively regulate employee conduct? The antecedents of rule following in work settings. *American Management Journal*, 48, 1143–1158

Van Dyne, L., & LePine, J.A. (1998). Helping and voice extra-role behaviour: Evidence of construct and predictive validity. *Academy of Management Journal*

Van Dyne, L., Cummings, L.L., & McLean Parks, J. (1995). Extra-Role behaviours: In pursuit of construct and definitional clarity. In L.L. Cummings & B.M. Stow (Eds.), *Research in Organizational Behaviour*

Vey, M.A., & Campbell, J.P. (2004). In-role or extra-role organizational citizenship behaviour: Which are we measuring? *Human Performance*, 17(1), 119–135

Walster, E., & Piliavin, J.A. (1972). Equity and the innocent bystander. *Journal of Social Issues*, 28(3), 165–189

Williams, L.J., & Anderson, S.E. (1991). Job satisfaction and organizational commitment as predictors of organizational citizenship and in-role behaviours. *Journal of Management*, 17, 601–617

Wispé, L.G. (1972). Positive forms of social behaviour: An overview. *Journal of Social Issues*, 28, 1–19. PsycINFO

Yankelovich, D., & Immerwahr, J. (1984). Putting the work ethic to work. *Society*, 21(2), 58–77

ABOUT THE AUTHORS

Marc Woods is a motivational speaker, modern-day adventurer, and multi-Gold medal winning Paralympic swimmer. He is the founding partner of management and leadership consultants SladenWoods, and author of the best-selling *Personal Best*. He also does media work for the BBC. When not working, he is often to be found in far-flung and dangerous places, or scraping the moss from the paving slabs in his garden.

Steve Coomber writes for *the Times*, and for various business publications. He has also worked with numerous organisations, many of them well-known, as a consultant or in a writing capacity of some sort. When not working, he is often to be found supporting Tottenham Hotspur, running slowly, or playing the guitar badly. Usually not at the same time.

INDEX

Index

Index